Word 5

by Adam Greif

WORD 5

Author

Adam Greif believes that books about the Macintosh should be as simple and visual as the Macintosh interface and programs. After writing eighteen such books in France (the *MacFacile* series, published in Paris by Dunod), he is now the editor and main author of Computer Generation's *Black Mouse* series.

ISBN 1 873469 03 9

Published by Computer Generation Ltd
3 Adam & Eve Mews
London W8 6UG

Tel: 071-937 8777 - Fax: 071-937 9487

UK trade distribution by Lund Humphries Publishers Ltd,

Park House, 1 Russell Gardens, London NW1T 9NN

Contents

The step-by-step visual approach of this book will help you learn Microsoft Word quickly and efficiently.
If you find it difficult to remember the details of the program's many functions, do not worry, just keep this book in your drawer.
Its simple and clear organization guarantees a smooth retrieval of any information.

If you are a complete Macintosh beginner, you should also read the Macintosh manuals so as to understand the role of files, folders, menu commands, etc.

This book describes Word 5.
You can also use it if you need to study Word 4 as *Basics* have not changed that much.

PRELIMINARY

There are three ways to install Word 5 - *easy, custom* and *lucky.*

If you work in a company and somebody else has already installed Word 5 on your Macintosh, then you're *lucky.* You may skip this page!

The *easy* way installs all the files on 5.5 MB of your hard disk, but the installation process itself requires 5 MB more.

See below how much space you might save either by *custom*-installing the program without some files, like *Grammar,* or by going the *easy*-install route and then throwing away files like *WordPerfect for DOS 5.x* if you don't need them.

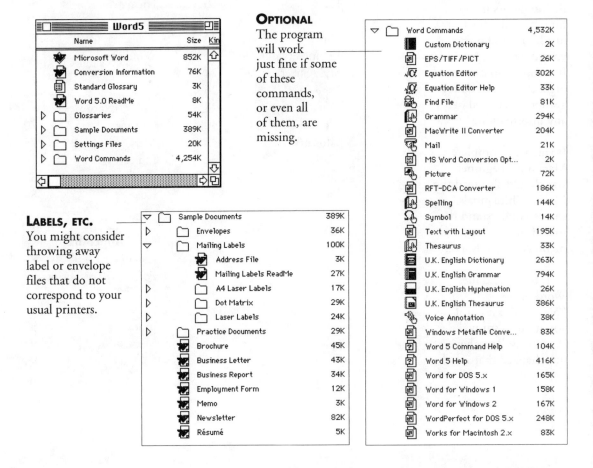

OPTIONAL
The program will work just fine if some of these commands, or even all of them, are missing.

LABELS, ETC.
You might consider throwing away label or envelope files that do not correspond to your usual printers.

Word5	Name	Size	Kin
	Microsoft Word	852K	
	Conversion Information	76K	
	Standard Glossary	3K	
	Word 5.0 ReadMe	8K	
▷	Glossaries	54K	
▷	Sample Documents	389K	
▷	Settings Files	20K	
▷	Word Commands	4,254K	

Sample Documents		389K
▷	Envelopes	36K
▽	Mailing Labels	100K
	Address File	3K
	Mailing Labels ReadMe	27K
▷	A4 Laser Labels	17K
▷	Dot Matrix	29K
▷	Laser Labels	24K
▷	Practice Documents	29K
	Brochure	45K
	Business Letter	43K
	Business Report	34K
	Employment Form	12K
	Memo	3K
	Newsletter	82K
	Résumé	5K

Word Commands		4,532K
	Custom Dictionary	2K
	EPS/TIFF/PICT	26K
	Equation Editor	302K
	Equation Editor Help	33K
	Find File	81K
	Grammar	294K
	MacWrite II Converter	204K
	Mail	21K
	MS Word Conversion Opt...	2K
	Picture	72K
	RFT-DCA Converter	186K
	Spelling	144K
	Symbol	14K
	Text with Layout	195K
	Thesaurus	33K
	U.K. English Dictionary	263K
	U.K. English Grammar	794K
	U.K. English Hyphenation	26K
	U.K. English Thesaurus	386K
	Voice Annotation	38K
	Windows Metafile Conve...	83K
	Word 5 Command Help	104K
	Word 5 Help	416K
	Word for DOS 5.x	165K
	Word for Windows 1	158K
	Word for Windows 2	167K
	WordPerfect for DOS 5.x	248K
	Works for Macintosh 2.x	83K

We fully endorse the computer industry's "Don't copy that floppy" campaign. Giving away or accepting a copy of a computer program is forbidden by law.

This book is not written for people who use a pirated copy of Word 5 without manuals.

It is written for people who own a legitimate program but find the 1,000+ pages of the manuals somewhat frightening, or for people who share one Macintosh, one Word 5 and one set of manuals with several colleagues in an office and nobody knows where the manuals have been hidden!

Keep this book handy to get acquainted quickly with Word 5 and to refresh your memory every now and then.

BASICS

A double-click on the Word 5 icon opens a new blank document called *Untitled1*. "Unnamed" would describe the state of the document better. When you save it, you are requested to give it a name rather than a title.

If you accept the default settings and begin to type immediately, your text may look like the one below – left-justified, single line spacing, no first line indents, etc.

In America, the default paper size is 8.5 x 11", with 1.25" left/right margins and 1" top/bottom margins. The example below corresponds to European A4 paper, which is 8.25" wide. The maximum width of the text is 5.75".

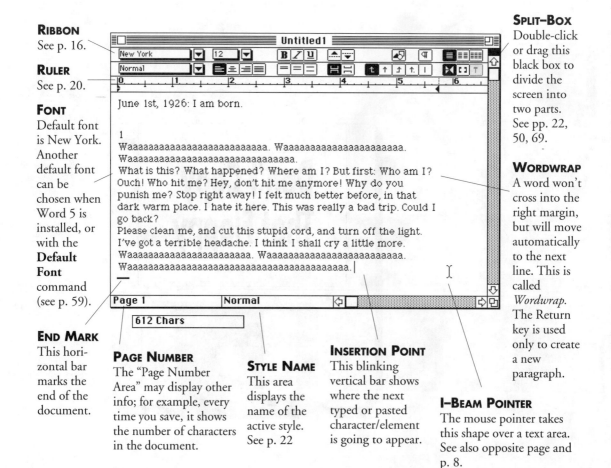

RIBBON
See p. 16.

RULER
See p. 20.

FONT
Default font is New York. Another default font can be chosen when Word 5 is installed, or with the **Default Font** command (see p. 59).

END MARK
This horizontal bar marks the end of the document.

PAGE NUMBER
The "Page Number Area" may display other info; for example, every time you save, it shows the number of characters in the document.

STYLE NAME
This area displays the name of the active style.
See p. 22

INSERTION POINT
This blinking vertical bar shows where the next typed or pasted character/element is going to appear.

SPLIT–BOX
Double-click or drag this black box to divide the screen into two parts.
See pp. 22, 50, 69.

WORDWRAP
A word won't cross into the right margin, but will move automatically to the next line. This is called *Wordwrap*. The Return key is used only to create a new paragraph.

I–BEAM POINTER
The mouse pointer takes this shape over a text area. See also opposite page and p. 8.

The picture below shows the document at a later stage. It is named *Marilyn* – its title is *I, Marilyn*. The margins and other attributes of the text have been changed.

As the New York font doesn't print well on a LaserWriter, it has been changed to Futura Bold for the Header and to Garamond for the main text. Garamond is a beautiful classical font (used for this book), but it is much harder to read on the screen than New York which was designed especially for the 72 dots per inch display of the Macintosh. You can't have everything – you must choose between eye comfort and aesthetics.

HEADER

When a page has a Header, it usually contains elements common to all the pages, like a title and a page number.
In Normal view, the Header is hidden (see left page, and also p. 22). In this example, the document is displayed in "Page Layout view."

SPECIAL POINTER

The I-Beam pointer reverts to the usual arrow shape (which points left) when you move it to the menu bar or to the scroll bars.
This right-facing pointer is a very special Word invention: it is used to select text (see p. 11).

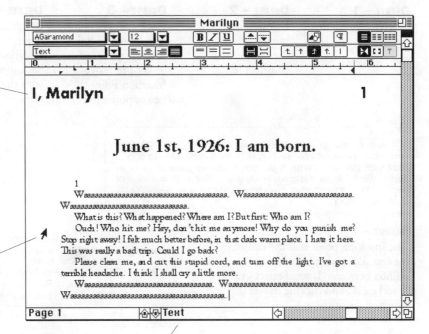

STYLE

A "Style" is a set of attributes used to format a text. Here, a style called Text has been created. Its attributes can be seen above: Garamond font, justified text, left margin 0.5" and first line indent 0.75", etc. Creating and using styles is explained on p. 22.

BASICS

The main difference between a word processing computer and a typewriter does not lie in the way you write, but rather in the way you edit and format what you write.

The I-Beam pointer lets you put the Insertion Point anywhere. You can then delete or insert text.

These techniques are not specific to Word, like the ones described on the opposite page, but work throughout the Macintosh universe.

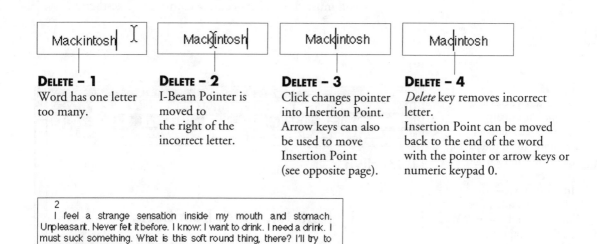

DELETE – 1
Word has one letter too many.

DELETE – 2
I-Beam Pointer is moved to the right of the incorrect letter.

DELETE – 3
Click changes pointer into Insertion Point. Arrow keys can also be used to move Insertion Point (see opposite page).

DELETE – 4
Delete key removes incorrect letter.
Insertion Point can be moved back to the end of the word with the pointer or arrow keys or numeric keypad 0.

2
I feel a strange sensation inside my mouth and stomach. Unpleasant. Never felt it before. I know: I want to drink. I need a drink. I must suck something. What is this soft round thing, there? I'll try to suck it. Wow! This liquid is good. Really good. What is it? Ambrosia or nectar, maybe. It was perfect.|I feel great, and also quite sleepy. Yeah, I shall sleep now.|

INSERT – 1
The Insertion point is at the end of the text. Positioning the I-Beam pointer between "It was perfect" and "I feel great" and clicking moves the Insertion point there.

2
I feel a strange sensation inside my mouth and stomach. Unpleasant. Never felt it before. I know: I want to drink. I need a drink. I must suck something. What is this soft round thing, there? I'll try to suck it. Wow! This liquid is good. Really good. What is it? Ambrosia or nectar, maybe. It was perfect. Best-tasting drink in my whole life.|I feel great, and also quite sleepy. Yeah, I shall sleep now.

INSERT – 2
A new sentence, "Best-tasting drink in my whole life.," has been typed in the middle of the text. The Insertion point can be moved back to the end of the text with the I-Beam pointer or by pressing the numeric keypad 0 key.

In Word, you can use the numeric keypad to move the Insertion point. People who don't know this are sometimes quite puzzled when they try to type numbers; not only do they see no number on the screen, but the Insertion Point seems to vanish mysteriously. You can still write numbers with the main keyboard, of course.

If you really want to type numbers with the numeric keypad, press the *Clear/Num Lock* key. The words Num Lock are then displayed in the Page Number area. You can still move the Insertion point with the arrow keys, which are rather more convenient than 2, 4, 6 and 8, but you lose the very useful "**Go Back**" function of the 0 key, which sends the Insertion Point to its last three locations.

NUM LOCK
Press this key to replace these functions with a real numeric keypad.

Num Lock		
7 Beginning of line	8 or ↑ Up one line	9 Top of window with scroll
4 or ← Previous character	5	6 or → Next character
1 End of line	2 or ↓ Down one line	3 Bottom of window with scroll

0
Go Back Insertion Point returns to where it was before.

⌘ **WITH COMMAND KEY**

7 Previous sentence	8 or ↑ Beginning of paragraph	9 Beginning of document
4 or ← Previous word	5 Top of window no scroll	6 or → Next word
1 Next sentence	2 or ↓ Next paragraph	3 End of document

BASICS

There are several levels of formatting in Word. You can format a document, a paragraph, or a string of characters.

When you want to delete, replace, move or reformat some characters, you must tell the program what portion of text is to be considered. This is done by "selecting" it.

Pressing the Delete key deletes whatever text is selected. Typing anything replaces the selected text with the new text. See p. 12 on how to move the selected text.

The left page (below) shows standard Macintosh selection techniques. The right page presents other methods, all of them specific to Word 5.

SELECTION

Selected text – also called "the selection" – is inverted (negative).

To select a short to medium-sized portion of text, click at one end, and drag the I-Beam Pointer to the other end. If the beginning of the selected text is near the bottom of the window and if you drag downward, the window scrolls automatically.

To select a long text, position the Insertion Point at one end, then move the I-Beam Pointer to the other end (this can involve scrolling) and Shift-click, i.e. press the Shift key and click.

FONT

The New York font (p. 6) looks good on the screen but doesn't print on the LaserWriter. Garamond (p. 7) and Helvetica (p. 8) are hard to read on the screen. This is Palatino, which is legible and prints well. Try it!

3

I have made an amazing discovery: when I open my eyes, I can see around me. There are two of these round things with the delicious liquid inside them, I think. They belong to a strange being with a pleasant voice and red hair. Unfortunately, I don't understand what he or she says.

pleasant voice and red hair. Oh I'm so sad: I just can't understand what he or she says.

He doesn't understand me, either. I must put more tone and variety into my waaaas.

BY THE WAY

This dotted line marks the end of a page and the beginning of a new one ("Automatic Page Break") in *Normal* view.

If you want to see the actual bottom and top of the pages, with Footer and Header, switch to *Page Layout* view (see p. 27).

ONE WORD

Double-click a word to select it. This is a very common technique. It happens often that one word is selected to be emphasized by italics or bold characters, or to be marked in the index-making process (see p. 53).

Select

The "selection bar" is an invisible vertical zone located between the text and the left border of the window. When the pointer moves to this bar, it becomes a right-facing arrow. See below how you can use this special pointer to select text.

As described on p. 9, the arrow keys and the numeric keypad let you move the Insertion Point around the screen. When you keep the Shift key down, this selects text between the old location of the Insertion Point and the new one.

ONE LINE
Click selection-bar pointer.

> He doesn't understand me, either. I must put more tone and heart into my waaaas.
> After a while, I could recognize a few objects and people. But then the strange being took me away suddenly. We stepped into a noisy

SEVERAL LINES
Drag pointer.

> the strange being took me away suddenly. We stepped into a noisy machine. It moved by itself. I was scared and cried a lot.
> Now we live in a small house. There are only three or four people

ONE PARAGRAPH
Double-click pointer.

> machine. It moved by itself. I was scared and cried a lot.
> Now we live in a small house. There are only three or four people around. When they see the person with the pleasant voice and the two round things, they say "Gladys". What does it mean?

WHOLE TEXT
Command-click or triple-click pointer. Also: choose **Select All** command in **Edit** menu (see p. 44).

> I recognize some words: Baby is wet; Baby wants milk; nice Baby. They say Baby a lot, and also something like Nomadji or Normandy which I don't understand. I still can say only waaaaaa.
> I love to drink milk from these round things. But sometimes the

ONE SENTENCE
Command-click or triple-click inside sentence.

> I love to drink milk from these round things. But sometimes the round things are replaced by a bottle with a rubber hat. The milk doesn't taste the same. It tastes lousy. Why do they punish me?

> 5
> Something horrible has happened. Gladys is gone. One day she was there, and the next day she had disappeared. Where is she? She has taken her two round things with her. Now I must drink from the bottle all the time. The situation is bad, and getting worse.

> 5
> Somet there, an taken he bottle all

> 5
> *Somet th ere an tak en he bo ttle all*

EXTEND TO
This peculiar technique was last mentioned in the Word 4 manuals, but still works in Word 5: press the minus (-) sign of the numeric keypad; the words **Extend to** appear in the page number area; typing a character (in this example: "?") selects text between the Insertion Point and the first occurence of the character.

ONE COLUMN
You can select a rectangle by pressing the Option key and dragging. This is useful when you want to change paragraph numbers to bold, etc.

ITALICS
Selected (and "half-selected") letters have been changed to Italics. This picture shows a great Word invention: slanted Insertion Point and I-Beam Pointer.

BASICS

As before, the left page shows how to move selected text the traditional Macintosh way, and the right page shows the exclusive Word 5 ways.

In the traditional way, the selected text is "cut" or "copied," then "pasted" either elsewhere inside the document or into another document.

The new Word 5 *Drag-and-Drop* method will only move text inside the document.

SELECT
A, B and C represent texts of any length; B and C belong to the same document.
Text A is to be moved between B and C.
First step is to select text A .

CUT
Cut command in Edit menu is chosen. Text A disappears into a special memory called the Clipboard (where it replaces whatever was cut or copied before).
If you worry easily, you can keep track of A by choosing the Show Clipboard command in the Window menu.

MOVE INSERTION POINT
Insertion Point is moved between text B and text C.

PASTE
When the Paste command in Edit menu is chosen, text A appears between B and C.
It stays in the Clipboard and can thus be pasted several times in different places.
If A was copied rather than cut, the sequence would be: ABC, A|BC, AB|C, ABAC.
If you want to be absolutely sure that A won't be lost between Cut and Paste due to a power failure or something, go the Copy way, then delete the old A:
ABC, A|BC, AB|C, ABAC, BAC.

FORMAT
Cut or copied text keeps its character and paragraph formatting when pasted inside Word, but may lose them when pasted into another program.

The first Word 5 method lets you simply drag-and-drop a selection to another location. This is great if you don't need to move the text very far or to another document.

The second and third methods involve "hidden commands," **Move Text** and **Copy Text**. These commands can be added to the **Edit** menu (see **Command...**, p. 84), but you can always access them via their shortcuts, Command-Option-X and C.

There is a fourth method. You can move whole paragraphs in **Outline** view (see p. 70).

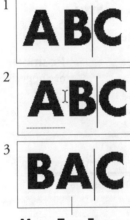

DRAG-AND-DROP

1. Move the I-Beam pointer to the selection; it should take the Arrow shape. Press the mouse button; the selection wobbles slightly and a dotted box appears at the bottom of the pointer.
2. Drag the pointer to the new location; it drives a dotted Insertion Point.
3. Releasing the mouse button moves the selection.

MOVE TEXT FROM

1. Put the Insertion Point between **B** and **C**.
Press Command-Option-X (or C if you want to copy). The words **Move from** appear in the Page Number area.
2. Drag over **A** with the I-Beam pointer. The text is not inverted, but marked by a dotted underline.
3. Press the Enter key to move **A** between **B** and **C**.

MOVE TEXT TO

1. Select text **A**. Press Command-Option-X (or C if you want to copy). The words **Move to** appear in the Page Number area.
2. Click between B and C; a dotted Insertion Point appears.
3. Press the Enter key to move **A** between **B** and **C**.

OUTLINE VIEW

"Collapsed" paragraphs are reduced to their first line. Dragging the square dots moves the paragraphs.

13

BASICS

The "ribbon" has a double role. It displays useful information about your text and lets you change its format with a few clicks.

The formats you can check and change with the left part of the ribbon are "character formats." They apply to any number of characters that you have selected or will type from now on. More character formats are accessed from the **Format** and **Font** menus.

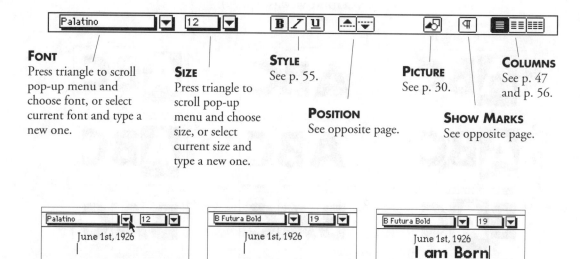

FONT
Press triangle to scroll pop-up menu and choose font, or select current font and type a new one.

SIZE
Press triangle to scroll pop-up menu and choose size, or select current size and type a new one.

STYLE
See p. 55.

POSITION
See opposite page.

PICTURE
See p. 30.

SHOW MARKS
See opposite page.

COLUMNS
See p. 47 and p. 56.

CHANGE CHARACTER FORMAT FOR FUTURE TEXT
The first line has been typed in Palatino 12. Format is changed to Futura Bold 19. New Format applies to what is typed until format is changed again.
Notice that size 19 can't be chosen in the menu, but must be entered by selecting 12 in the box and replacing it.

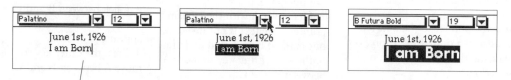

CHANGE CHARACTER FORMAT FOR EXISTING TEXT
Two lines have been typed in Palatino 12. Second line is selected. Format is changed to Futura Bold 19. New Format applies to selection and to what will be typed after it.

If you do not write for publication, or if somebody proof-reads your text after you, just skip this page.

If you proof-read your own text or whoever's, you must be very careful about small details like Superscript and Subscript characters. Word 5 doesn't reduce their size automatically.

Showing the marks lets you track mistakes like double spaces.

SUPERSCRIPT/SUBSCRIPT
"7" has been selected and the Superscript button has been clicked. The character moves up 3 pt. Same thing for "8" and Subscript (down 2 pt).
"235" and "2" have been moved down and up *and* reduced in size. This can be done in two steps: click Super- or Subscript button and reduce size, or in one step: press Command-Shift and Plus (or Minus) sign when "Num Lock" is on.

> Add $^7/_8$ pure U$_{235}$ and remember: E = mc^2

TABULATION MARK
Tab key.

PARAGRAPH MARK
Return key.

bottle·all·the·time.·The·situation·is·bad,·and·getting·worse.¶
→   There·are·two·persons.·One·has·a·pleasant·voice·like·
Gladys.·Her·name·is·Ida.·The·other·one·has·a·much·lower·voice,↵
some-what·frightening.·Albert-Hen·seems·to·be·her·name.·They·also·
talk·often·of·a·certain·"Jesus",·but·I·haven't·seen·her·yet.¶
One·thing·worries·me:·they·insist·on·calling·me·Norm adjin.·Could·
this·be·my·name?·How·ugly!·They·should·at·least·consult·you·↵
before·they·give·you·a·name.·I·hope·that·Gladys·will·come·back·and·
take·me·away·from··here.¶
¶

LINE BREAK
(A.k.a *Soft Return*).
Art directors often like to alternate shorter and longer lines in left-justified text. This is done by pressing Shift-Return, which starts a new line but not a new paragraph.

OPTIONAL HYPHEN
This Command-Hyphen in the middle of "somewhat" is visible only when the *Show Marks* option is on. It means the word could break there at the end of a line.

DOUBLE SPACE
Use the Find/Replace function (see p. 45) to replace double space by single one.

NON-BREAKING HYPHEN
Command-Tilde puts a "non-breaking" hyphen in the middle of Albert-Hen. It means that the word won't break at the end of a line, but will move whole to the next line.

NON-BREAKING SPACE
Option- or Command-Spacebar puts a "non-breaking" space in the middle of Norm adjin. It means that the two words won't be separated at the end of a line, but will move whole to the next line.

15

BASICS

The ruler is a convenient tool for rough paragraph formatting. Choices made on the ruler apply either to the *current* or *active* paragraph (i.e. the paragraph where the Insertion Point blinks) and the following paragraphs until other choices are made, or to the selected paragraph(s).

The formatting of a paragraph is "kept" by the program in the ¶ mark at the end of the paragraph. If you delete this mark (you can click the ¶ button on the Ribbon to see the mark, but you can also select it when it is not visible: try it!), the paragraph loses its formatting and takes the formatting of the next paragraph.

Double-clicking an Alignment/Line Spacing/Paragraph Spacing button or choosing the **Paragraph...** command in the **Format** menu opens the *Paragraph* dialog box (see p. 18), which gives you more, and more precise, formatting choices.

STYLE SHEET
Click on triangle to scroll pop-up menu, or select style name and type another one. See p. 22.

ALIGNMENT
This paragraph is left-aligned (or "left-justified").

This paragraph is centered.

This one is right-aligned (or "right-justified").

This paragraph is justified (or "fully justified"). See opposite page.

LINE SPACING
Left button (default) sets line spacing to "auto," i.e. font size plus two points. Middle button sets it to 18 pt (no action if font size is bigger), right button to 24 pt (same restriction). See p. 18.

PARAGRAPH SPACING
No blank line between paragraphs (default), or one blank line. See p. 18.

TAB STOPS
Clicking on the ruler when one of these buttons is selected creates the corresponding tab stop. See p. 20.

THREE RULERS
The left (default) button displays this ruler. The middle button displays a ruler with "margin brackets" (see p. 28), the right button a ruler for tables (see p. 34).

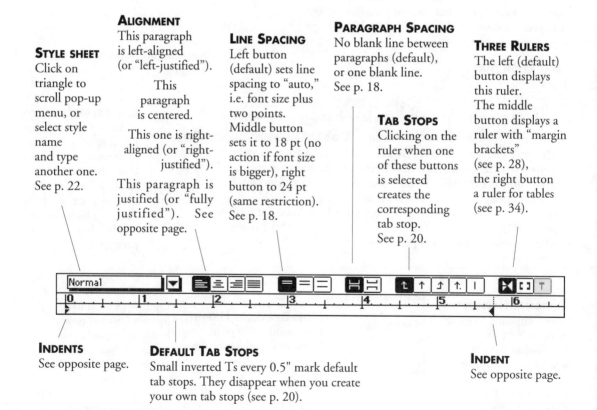

INDENTS
See opposite page.

DEFAULT TAB STOPS
Small inverted Ts every 0.5" mark default tab stops. They disappear when you create your own tab stops (see p. 20).

INDENT
See opposite page.

16

When you drag a little indent triangle, its distance to the margin is displayed in the Page Number area. Thus, you can control its movement. This method is fine if you want to drop it at 0.5, 0.75, 1.0 or 1.5", etc., and also at some places in-between. Use the **Paragraph...** command in the **Format** menu if you want maximum precision.

The triangles are stopped by the margin but if you insist, they move into the margin and a negative distance is displayed.

You should be very careful when trying to justify text in narrow columns. See below.

> I've improved my waas. I can modulate and be very expressive.
> Also, I can now say "Ma". The two persons are quite impressed with my "Ma". The first time I said it, they applauded. I like applause. But then, the person with the

> applauded. I like applause. But then, the person with the pleasant voice said:
> "I'm not your Ma. Gladys is your Ma, Normadjin. I'm your Onteyeda."
> Actually, Gladys comes once a week. We go to a big house together. A person there talks

> Actually, Gladys comes once a week. We go to a big house together.
> A person there talks about this mysterious Jesus like Ida and Albert-Hen.
> I don't hear right yet. I'm not sure that Albert-Hen's name is Albert-Hen. Could be

> • A person there talks about this mysterious Jesus like Ida and Albert-Hen.
> • I don't hear right yet. I'm not sure that Albert-Hen's name is Albert-When. Could be Albert-When.
> • There is no more milk in the two round things.

FIRST-LINE INDENT
Drag the upper triangle ("first-line indent marker") for this traditional layout.

INDENTED PARAGRAPH
Drag the lower triangle ("left-indent marker") to indent whole active paragraph.
The upper triangle follows when you drag.

HANGING INDENTS
Shift-Drag the lower triangle to move it without the upper one. You could also move both triangles, then drag the upper one left.

BULLETS
Set hanging indent.
Type bullet (or number, etc.).
Press Tab key to align first word with the rest of the paragraph.

> 7
> A new person has arrived. Her name is Della, but Gladys calls her Ma. It does not make sense. She lives across the street. She takes me to her house and calls me "My baby, my sweet Normadjin,   my   pretty granddaughter". I don't like her voice.

JUSTIFIED
Word 5 aligns justified text by increasing space between words. The line "Normadjin, my pretty" doesn't look too good.
If the column is not too narrow, you can improve things by hyphenating grand–daughter yourself, or by asking the program to do it (see p. 65).

> She takes me to her house and calls me "My baby, my sweet Normadjin,   my granddaughter". I don't like her voice.

WIDE SPACE
Two words fill a line, with an enormous space between them.

SHORT LINE
One word stays by itself.

> She takes me to her house and calls me "Omybaby, Omysweet Normadjin, Omyprettygranddaughter".   I don't like her voice.

Spacing is always measured in points, but you can write 0.5 in or 0.5 cm. The program will convert it to points. You can also write numbers followed by cm or pt in the Indentation boxes and they will be converted to inches (or whatever default unit you have chosen in the *Preferences* dialog box – see p. 66).

Click Apply to see what the formatting looks like – you can move the dialog box if it hides the paragraph – then confirm your choice by clicking OK.

PARAGRAPH SPACING

This lets you mark the space between paragraphs by less than a line (in the example below, 6 pt). You can also put a lot of space before and after a paragraph/a picture to isolate it.

LINE SPACING

See opposite page.

INDENTATION

For a x" hanging indent, enter x in the *Left* box, and -x in the *First* box. If x is 0.5, you can set the hanging indent with the shortcut Shift-Command-T.

TABS...

Clicking one of these buttons opens the corresponding dialog box on top of the paragraph one.

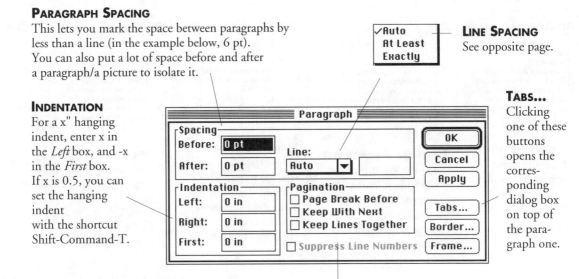

There's this other baby, Lesta. Della does not take it to her house and does not call it "My sweet Lesta". Why?

I am afraid of Della. Once, in her house, she put a pillow on my face and I could not breathe. Then she said: "Oh, my poor sweet Normadjin, what was I doing? I am crazy. Oh forgive me my darling... Oh Lord Jesus, please Jesus, forgive a poor sinner..."

PAGINATION

Dotted line indicates a page break in the middle of the paragraph at left. Notice 6 pt spacing before paragraph.

When the *Page Break Before* box is checked, the dotted line moves before the paragraph. This is like a manual page break, and should be used for a new chapter, etc.

Keep With Next avoids a break between two paragraphs.

Keep Lines Together avoids breaking the paragraph when it is near the bottom of the page, either by sending it to the next page, or by allowing more lines in the page.

Word doesn't break paragraphs after their first line or before their last line. This can be overruled (if you want a fixed number of lines per page) in the *Document* dialog box. See p. 28.

Line Spacing is also called linespacing or linespace or, if you want to sound really professional, leading (pronounced *ledding*, because type used to be made of lead). Many Macintosh programs set automatic line spacing at 120% of the font size or so. Word 5 *doesn't*, but adds 2 pt to the size: Auto leading is 14 pt for a standard 12 pt font, 26 pt for a 24 pt font, etc.

Automatic line spacing is OK for everyday use. If you are interested in readability and aesthetics, you should try custom leading. A smaller font with increased leading may read better in some cases.

This text is set in Garamond 11 with a leading of 12 only. This is usually abbreviated to Garamond 11/12. It doesn't seem cramped because the font has a small "x-height" (or body).

JUNE 1st, 1926: I AM BORN.

JUNE 1st, 1926: I AM BORN.

Auto: 18/20
Art Directors often reduce leading for titles in caps. This is size 18 Futura Bold with auto (i.e. 20) leading. See reduction on the right.

Exactly: 18/18
If there was no comma, leading could go down to 16. With a title in lower case, you should choose a smaller leading when there are no descenders (i.e. g or p or y) in the first line/no ascenders (b, d, f, etc.) in the second line.

Della tried to kill me another time. She took me to the house of this invisible Jesus, and there she threw me into a pool of water. "Now you are baptized in the name of the **Lord Jesus**, Normadjin", she said. I was lucky: there was a person who rescued me. I could have drowned. I cried a lot.

Della tried to kill me another time. She took me to the house of this invisible Jesus, and there she threw me into a pool of water. "Now you are baptized in the name of the **Lord Jesus**, Normadjin", she said. I was lucky: there was a person who rescued me. I could have drowned. I cried a lot.

At least 18
When you click the middle linespacing button on the ruler, you get "at least 18" leading. You can also choose **At Least** in the *Spacing* pop-up menu and write a number. The program then increases leading to accomodate bigger fonts.

Exactly 18
If you choose **Exactly** in the pop-up menu and enter a number, a bigger font won't increase leading. Tall letters may be cropped when leading is not big enough.

19

BASICS

To set a tab stop on the ruler, just choose a type by clicking one of the tab buttons (default is Left tab), then click where you want the tab stop to appear. This suppresses all the default tab stops located to the left of the new one.

You can drag your tab stop along the ruler and control its distance to the left margin in the Page Number area.

To suppress a tab stop, drag it above or under the ruler.

You should remember that the tab settings affect the active paragraph and stay on if you type new paragraphs after it. If you want to change the settings of several existing paragraphs, you must select them together first.

Screen	6	Screen	6
Edit	8	Edit	8
Select	10	Select	10
Move	12	Move	12

Left (Default)
A Left tab stop is set at 5.5". When you write a word and press the tab key, the Insertion Point moves to 5.5" and the page number you write is left-aligned on 5.5".

Right (Better)
A Right tab stop is set at 5.5". When you write a word and press the tab key, the Insertion Point moves to 5.5" and the page number you write is right-aligned on 5.5".

Leader
If you have checked the dotted *Leader* button in the *Tabs* dialog box (see opposite page), a dotted line appears when you press the tab key.

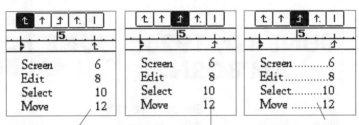

January	25.6	cold
February	8.45	very cold
March	41.4	cool
April	50.21	pleasant

Bar
This works without the tab key. When you click a bar mark onto the ruler, a vertical bar appears under it in the active paragraph or in the selected one(s).

Decimal
Decimal point is aligned under tab stop.

Center
When you press the tab key after writing a temperature number, what you type is centered around the 3.5" mark.

To open the *Tabs* dialog box, choose the **Tabs...** command in the **Format** menu, click the *Tabs...* button in the *Paragraph* dialog box or double-click a tab stop or tab button on the ruler. The dialog box lets you adjust the position of the tab stop precisely and choose a "Leader."

If you open the dialog box by double-clicking a tab stop, information about this tab stop appears inside the dialog box.

The tab functions of the ruler remain active while the Tabs dialog box is on. Thus you can select a tab stop on the ruler and move it, change its type by clicking a tab button or click on the ruler to set a new tab stop.

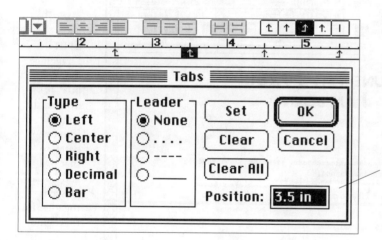

POSITION

The Position box gives you the same information about the selected tab stop as the Page Number area but you can, of course, enter numbers into it yourself and define the position of the tab stop very precisely.
The choices you make inside this dialog box are saved when you click Set or OK.

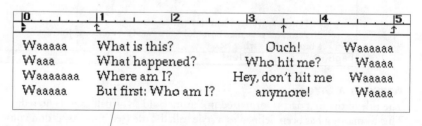

HAIKU

You can juxtapose small poems or whatever in this way, but creating a table would be more convenient than using tabs. See p. 34.

BASICS

Styles are considered one of the major contributions of Word to the word processing and DTP world. In fact, when a new program is described, you'll often read that "it has (or doesn't have) styles like Word's."

Styles are especially useful if you write technical documents with several levels of titles/subtitles/headings, etc. You would then assign a style to each level.

Styles also play a very important role in DTP programs like PageMaker or QuarkXPress. Understanding styles is a must if you plan to use Word 5 for DTP.

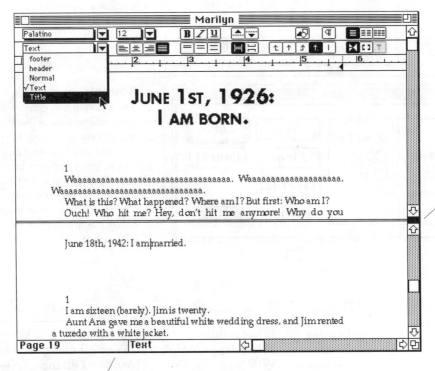

SPLIT
Dragging the "split-box" has divided the window into two parts, so that p. 1 and 19 can be seen together for this demo.

APPLYING A STYLE

The title of the first part is formatted in Futura Bold 24, small caps, centered. This formatting has been defined as a style called Title (see how this is done on the opposite page). To apply the same attributes to the title of the second part, all you have to do is choose the command in the Style pop-up menu when the Insertion Point is inside the title.

Defining a Style

There are two main ways to define a style. The first one is explained here: format a paragraph with all the features you want (using ribbon, ruler and menu commands), then use the paragraph's formatting to define the style.

The second way starts with the **Style...** command of the **Format** menu. See next page.

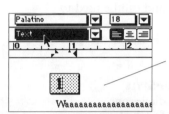

FORMAT A PARAGRAPH

A chapter number is a one character paragraph, here formatted with a bigger font and a "border." Notice that the border goes all the way to the right indent.

The paragraph being active, the style menu name (here, *Text*) is clicked and selected.

NAME A NEW STYLE

Typing *Number* to replace *Text* and pressing the Enter key displays this dialog box.

A new style named *Number* will be added to the style menu.

CHANGE AN EXISTING STYLE

Pressing the Enter key without replacing *Text* displays this dialog box. You can either revert the selection to its original *Text* style, or use the selection to change the *Text* style.

ADDITIONAL FORMATTING

In the paragraph below the chapter number, the first line indent, which is part of the *Text* style for *Marilyn*, has been removed for aesthetic reasons. The paragraph doesn't follow the exact *Text* style anymore and the Style Name area says *Text+...* instead of *Text*.

Clicking the pop-up menu style name would display the "Change an Existing Style" dialog box.

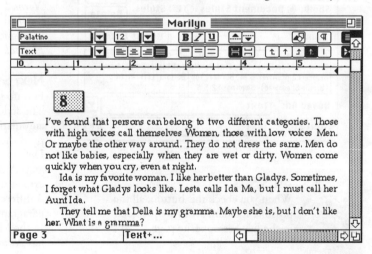

23

BASICS

You can work with styles without ever choosing the **Styles...** command and opening the dialog box below by sticking to the technique shown on the preceding page. The dialog box offers one big bonus: a full description of any style you select in the list.

The dialog box also lets you name and define a new style, or change an existing style. What you must remember (especially if you use other programs, like QuarkXPress, where the Style dialog box is different) is that, when the dialog box is on, the ribbon and ruler and menu commands all stay active and can be used to define the style.

The list of styles attached to a document is called the *Style Sheet* of this document.

NEW STYLE
Select this line, choose a name and define a new style with ribbon, ruler and menus.

STANDARD STYLE
A bullet indicates one of Word's Standard Styles (see opposite page).

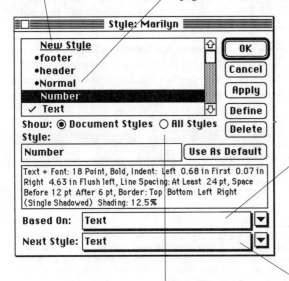

ALL STYLES
When you check this button, all the possible standard styles are included in the list. See opposite page.

BASED ON
Pop-up menu shows style sheet.
As the chapter numbers initially belonged to the *Text* style, the new *Number* style is "based on *Text*." This means that if you replace Palatino by Garamond in *Text*, it will also be replaced by Garamond in *Number*.
Text, like most of the styles, is itself based on *Normal*, which is basically the granddaddy of them all. So if you really want to replace a font throughout the text, you should change *Normal*.

NEXT STYLE
Pop-up menu shows style sheet.
The style you choose as *Next Style* is applied automatically to the next paragraph when you press the Return key after the active paragraph. Default *Next Style* for a paragraph is the paragraph's own style, as you want the style to extend to the next paragraph.
A different *Next Style* makes sense only if the paragraph is some kind of title.
In the Marilyn style sheet, for example, *Title* has *Number* as next style and *Number* has *Text*, but *Text* also has *Text*.

Style Sheet

The style sheet of a document can include: some of Word's standard styles (see below); styles you have created for this document; styles you import when you paste paragraphs cut or copied from another document; styles you import from another document by choosing the **Open...** command in the **File** menu when the style dialog box is on and "merging" the two style sheets; etc.

If you paste a paragraph formatted with a style called *Text* and if your document also has a *Text* style, the paragraph will lose its old format and adapt to its new environment. If you "merge" two style sheets with *Text* styles, it is the other way around. The incoming *Text* replaces your document's *Text* style.

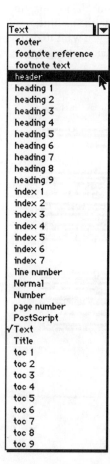

STANDARD STYLES
When you press the Shift key and scroll the Style pop-up menu, all the possible standard styles are displayed with the document's styles.
Choosing one of these styles puts it into the document's style sheet.
"toc" means "Table of Contents."

ALL STYLES
Checking the *All Styles* button is similar to Shift-scrolling the Style menu; all the standard styles are displayed.
You can change a standard style for the active document. If you want to change it for all new documents, click the *Use As Default* button. This button also lets you add a new style (like *Number*) to the default style sheet of all new documents.

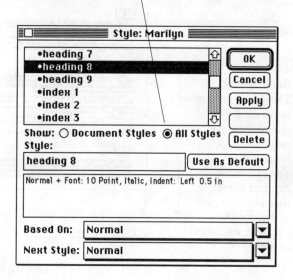

BASICS

A Word 5 page can include several "parts." You create a *Header* and/or *Footer* by choosing the **Header** and/or **Footer** command in the **View** menu. Footnotes also add parts to the page.

In the example below, there are two Headers and two Footers: even and odd. See how this is done on p. 29.

Whereas margins are defined for the whole document (see p. 28), you can divide a document into *Sections* and put different Headers and/or Footers in every section (see p. 56).

HEADER
The default location of a one-line Header is just inside the top margin. Here the header had several lines, so it overflows into the main text part. Choose the **Section...** command (see p. 56) if you want to define the location of the Header/Footer more precisely than by dragging.

PRINT PREVIEW
Choosing **Print Preview...** in the **File** menu displays a reduced view of the document where the Header and Footer can be moved (but not resized; see opposite page for size).
See also p. 28.

PAGE BREAK
The dotted line just above the Footer shows where the automatic page break occurs.
You can drag it up to create a "manual page break". Text under this line would be sent to the next page. Try it!

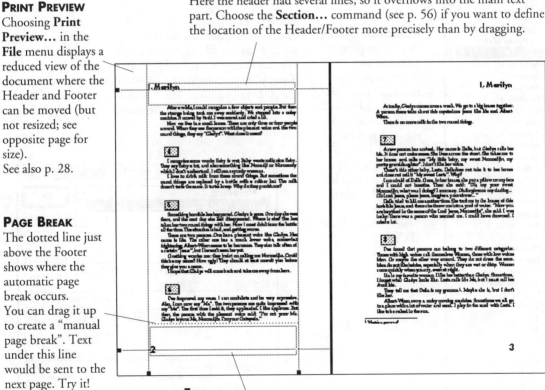

FOOTER
Like the Header, the Footer sits astride the text part and the margin.

In fully wysiwyg programs like MacWrite II, the Header and Footer are usually visible and reduce your working area.

In Word's *Normal* view they are hidden. When you choose **Header** or **Footer** in the **View** menu, the Header's (or Footer's) window is displayed. You can show ribbon and ruler inside this window, and format the Header (or Footer) any way you like. You adjust its width by dragging the indent marks, and its height by changing line spacing and adding/removing returns.

Page Number, etc.
Click an icon to drop page number, date or time after Insertion Point.

Header Style
Standard *Header* style has center tab stop at 3" and right tab stop at 6", i.e. in the margin (for page number).

Footnote Style
Standard *Footnote* style is based on *Normal*, with smaller characters.

Separator
This horizontal line has its own part and can be replaced by other symbols (see p. 50).

Footnote
You can choose to put the Footnote part at the bottom of the page, like here, or elsewhere (see p. 29).
Footnotes, like Headers/Footers, are hidden in *Normal* view.

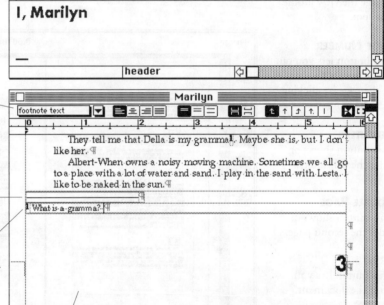

Page Layout
Page Layout view shows the page as it will print; you can't move parts or change margins like in *Print Preview*, but you can edit text.

BASICS

In *Print Preview* mode, the four margin delimiters have black square handles. You can drag them to change the margins for the whole document. While you drag, a measure appears at the top of the Preview box to help you adjust the position of the margin delimiter.

If a document has *Mirror Even/Odd* pages, like the one below, changing the margins on one side changes them on the other side automatically.

MAGNIFYER
This button changes the Pointer into a magnifyer. Click on a spot to enlarge the view around that spot.

PAGE NUMBER
This button lets you put a page number anywhere on the page by clicking, then dragging.

DELIMITERS
This button shows or hides the delimiters.

DOUBLE PAGE
This button shows or hides the second page.

PRINT
This button lets you print the document.

MARGIN BRACKETS
Dragging the ruler's "Margin Brackets" is another way to change the vertical margins.

LASERWRITER MARGIN
0.50" is the default for margins if you plan to print standard pages on a LaserWriter printer. *Larger Print Area* option lets you reduce the margin to 0.25" (see p. 42).

PAGE LAYOUT
This button displays the Page Layout view.

CLOSE
This button displays the Normal view.

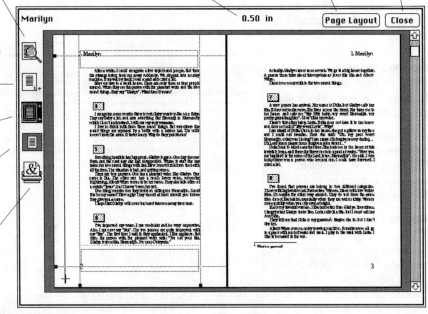

Document

The dialog box below, which you open by choosing the **Document...** command in the **Format** menu, shows choices you make for the whole document. Choices you make for a *Section*, e.g. Header/Footer location, can be seen on p. 56.

Other *Document* choices, e.g. paper size, document orientation, Graphics smoothing, are made in the traditional Macintosh **Page Setup** dialog box. See p. 42.

AT LEAST
Pop-up menus say **At Least** and **Exactly**.
At Least is the default option. A multiline Header/Footer pushes the main text down/up. Choose **Exactly** if you want the text to stay put so that a Header/Footer can "overlap" it. You could try this for a margin page number, for example.
The result is visible only in *Print Preview* mode.

MIRROR
When the *Mirror Even/Odd* button is checked, the *Left* and *Right* margins become *Inside* and *Outside*.

GUTTER
This is an extra inside margin to accomodate binding.

FOOTNOTES
Pop-up menu says **Bottom of Page**, **Beneath Text**, **End of Section**, **End of Document**. See also p. 56.

Document

Margins
Left: `1.25 in`   Top: `1 in`   `At Least ▼`
Right: `1.25 in`   Bottom: `1 in`   `At Least ▼`
Gutter: `0 in`   ☐ Mirror Even/Odd

Footnotes
Position: `Bottom of Page ▼`
○ Restart Each Page
◉ Number From: `1`

☒ Widow Control
☐ Print Hidden Text
☐ Even/Odd Headers
Default Tab Stops: `0.5 in`

`OK`
`Cancel`
`Use As Default`
`File Series...`

WIDOWS
This box is checked by default. Word avoids lonely lines before or after a page break. Uncheck it if you need pages with a fixed number of lines.

HIDDEN
"Hidden" is one of the possible styles of text (see p. 55). Usually, hidden text is shown on screen, but not printed.

FILE SERIES
Very long documents are easier to manage when divided into several smaller documents. This button lets you link the smaller documents. You can then print or index as if there was only one document.

BASICS

The Marilyn book actually belongs to a series of mock biographies. It has been decided to keep the title *I, Marilyn* in the Odd Header, but to put the series' name in the Even Header.

Adding a cute picture will obviously enhance the appeal of the book. Drawing the picture is the only tough part of the process… The black mouse was drawn in HyperCard, then copied. Then comes the easy part, putting the Insertion Point before the series' name and choosing the **Paste** command.

The picture appears after the Insertion Point exactly as if it was a regular character.

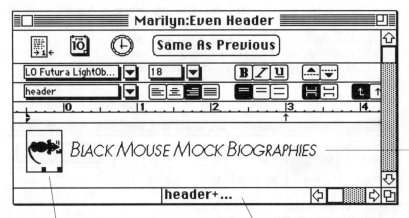

BASELINE
The bottom of the picture rests on the baseline. As the series' name wanted to keep abreast with the mouse, it was formatted as superscript and raised 15 pt (in the *Character* dialog box, see p. 55).
The title *I, Marilyn* should be raised by the same amount, in the Odd Header, for symmetry's sake.

HANDLES
The frame border and the three square handles appear when the picture is selected with a click.

MARGIN
The style reads header+… because a negative indent has been set to place the picture inside the margin.

CROPPING
Dragging the right/bottom handle changes the width/height of the picture's frame. Dragging the corner handle enlarges or reduces the frame proportionally. As the picture doesn't move, it may be "cropped."

SCALING
Shift-dragging a handle changes the picture with the frame. Here the picture has been enlarged to 200% of its size. The proportion is displayed in the Page Number area while you drag.

30

Picture

You can't really draw anything except simple geometric figures inside Word 5's *Insert Picture* window, but it is very convenient as a kind of halfway house where you resize, colour, rotate and group pasted pictures before importing them into your text.

OBJECTS

Select tool and drag to draw straight line, rectangle, oval or arc.
Polygon tool lets you click to define the corners of a polygon. Double-click on last corner.
Objects have eight handles, which can be dragged with arrow pointer.

ROTATION

See example below. Special pointer lets you rotate object. Angle is displayed at bottom of window.

LAYERS

Pop-up menu says **Bring to Front**, **Send to Back**. In example below, a grey square is drawn "in front" of a white one, then selected and sent to back.

ALIGNMENT

Pop-up menu says **Align** [text] **Left**, **Center** and **Right**.

COLOUR AND PATTERN

Pop-up menus show colours and patterns for lines and borders or to fill/colour the whole object.

PICTURE WINDOW

To open an empty window, click the *Picture* button on the ribbon, or choose the **Picture...** command in the **Insert** menu and click the *New Picture* button. When you close the window, all the pictures it contains are grouped and inserted as a single character at the Insertion Point.
If you want to edit this picture-character later on, double-click it to see it inside the window again.

TEXT TOOL

Select tool, then click to place Insertion Point or drag to define text frame.
Text can be edited, but few formatting options are available. It is often better to format text inside word processor, then "copy as graphic" (Option-Command-D) and paste inside Picture window.

DUPLICATE

Select object, then click this button to duplicate it.

MIRROR

Pop-up menu says **Flip Horizontal**, **Flip Vertical**.

LINE WIDTH

Pop-up menu offers a choice of widths for lines.

ARROWS

Straight line can become left, right or double arrow.

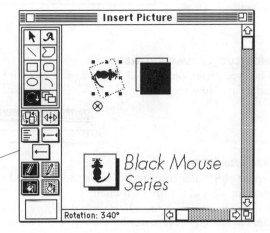

31

BASICS

A Glossary is a kind of library where you can keep frequently used words, texts, pictures, tables, etc.

When the *Glossary* dialog box is open, some commands of the **File** menu are available. You can **Open** another Glossary, or create a new one with the **New** and **Save as...** commands. You can also **Print** the Glossary. This doesn't just print the names of the entries, but their whole contents.

STANDARD
Bullets indicate standard Word 5 entries. *Date* doesn't change once inserted. *Print Date* (another standard entry, further down the list) is updated every time you print the document.

INSERT
Clicking this button inserts the selected entry (in this case, the *Black Mouse* picture) at the Insertion Point.
See below how this is done more conveniently through a shortcut.

DEFINE
There are two ways to add entries to the Glossary. You can either select some text/a picture/a table, then choose the **Glossary...** command, name the entry and click this button; or copy the text/picture/table, choose the **Glossary...** command, name the entry and choose the **Paste** command.

SAMPLE
The beginning of text entries is shown here (see opposite page). For a picture, all you get is a rectangle.

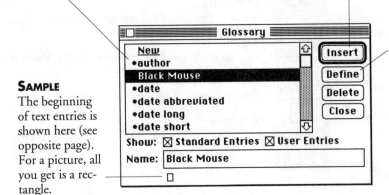

SHORTCUT: COMMAND-DELETE
When you press Command-Delete, the word *Name* is highlighted in the Page Number area.

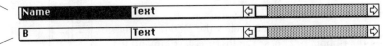

TYPE AND ENTER
Type the beginning of an entry's name and press the Enter key to insert the entry at the Insertion Point.
In this example, "B" is enough, as there is only one B word. Case does not matter. Creative naming ("ßlack M.") may save time.

A company logo, a 500 words copyright notice, are obvious glossary entry candidates. To set your imagination working, two more examples are given below.

The Word 5 manual recommends that the names of favorite glossary entries be put into the custom **Work** menu (see p. 84).

It also sees favorite *Glossaries* as good **Work** commands. You should be very careful about using several glossarie. When one glossary is open, choosing another glossary through the **Open…** command or through the **Work** menu doesn't open it beside the first one, but *merges* it into the first one. See below.

ANDRÉ

André de Dienes, a Hungarian photographer, played a very important part in Marilyn Monroe's early career. Putting his name in the glossary means that the bothersome é does not have to be typed every time André is mentioned in the story.

Similar example: Black Mouse®, etc.

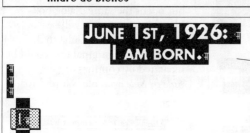

FORMATTING

When selecting an expression like André de Dienes to define it as a Glossary entry, you should be careful not to include any ¶ mark, as you probably want the name to adopt the formatting of the paragraph it will be inserted in.

In this example, ¶ marks are included in the selection. The entry will appear at the Insertion Point just as it is here. This is not very different from creating a *Title* style with *Number* as Next Style (see p. 25), but it does give you more informations; that there are three lines between title and number, that the date is not followed by a full stop but by a colon, etc.

OPEN ANOTHER GLOSSARY

Let's say you have added entries to the Standard Glossary. If you choose the **Open…** command and double-click *Formula Glossary*, the *Formula* entries are added to yours. If you just want the *Formula* entries without yours, you must first choose the **New** command and click *Yes* when this dialog box is displayed.

But wait! Before you do that, if your entries are freshly defined, do not forget to **Save** your personalised Standard Glossary!

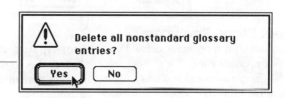

BASICS

The Word 5 manual suggests, "Why don't you import a table from Excel?" This is good advice (see p. 78), but actually, creating tables within Word is not as tough as it is reputed to be.

What is slightly unnerving is that there are commands in several menus: **Table…** in **Insert** (to create the table), **Table Cells…** and **Table Layout…** in **Format** (to format and modify it). You also need to choose **Border…** if you want lines between the cells.

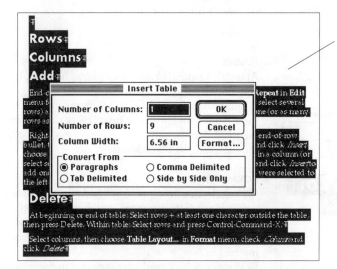

TEXT TO TABLE

The **Table…** command creates an empty table. You click into its "cells" and type. You can also move from a cell to another with Tab and Shift-Tab, like in a Spreadsheet program.

Here, nine paragraphs of text have been written first and selected. The command becomes **Text to Table**, but opens the same dialog box. Number of columns will be changed from 1 (default) to 3. Cell entries in original text could be separated by commas or tabs. *Side by Side* is an old Word 3 format.

APPLY

Formatting can be applied to selected cells, rows or columns containing selected cells, or the entire table.

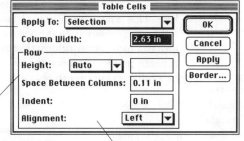

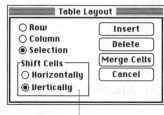

SHIFT CELLS

Inserting/deleting Rows and Columns is explained on the opposite page.

When you insert or delete a selected group of cells, you can choose to displace a similar group to the right of it (*Horizontally*) or under it (*Vertically*).

COLUMN WIDTH, ROW HEIGHT

Column width is more easily defined on ruler (see opposite page).

Row height can adjust to text (*Auto* or *At Least*) or not (*Exactly* – useful if you want a lot of white space, e.g. for forms).

INDENT, ALIGNMENT

This applies to the whole table relative to the page margins.

Tables

The text formatting of this table was done before it was created; mainly left and right indents and space before and after paragraphs, so there is some white between text and cell borders. You can also format text inside selected cells by reverting to the default ruler or using the usual formatting commands. When the table is created, the special Table ruler is on. It lets you change the width of cells and columns by dragging little Ts.

INDENT
This special Indent marker lets you indent (move horizontally) whole rows containing selected cells.

SELECT
There is a selection bar at the top of every column and at the left of every cell.
Cell selection is done with the usual right-arrow pointer, column selection with this down arrow.

WIDTH
Dragging a little T changes the width of selected cell(s). To change the width of a whole column, select it with the down arrow first. This was done here to narrow the left column, as a brand new table comes with equal columns.

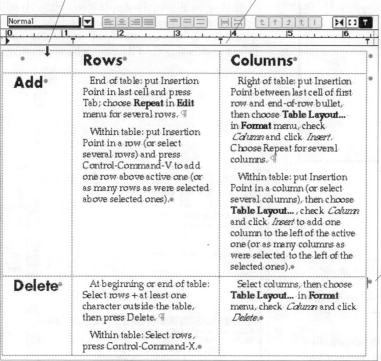

	Rows•	Columns•
Add•	End of table: put Insertion Point in last cell and press Tab; choose **Repeat** in **Edit** menu for several rows. ¶ Within table: put Insertion Point in a row (or select several rows) and press Control-Command-V to add one row above active one (or as many rows as were selected above selected ones).•	Right of table: put Insertion Point between last cell of first row and end-of-row bullet, then choose **Table Layout...** in **Format** menu, check *Column* and click *Insert*. Choose Repeat for several columns. ¶ Within table: put Insertion Point in a column (or select several columns), then choose **Table Layout...**, check *Column* and click *Insert* to add one column to the left of the active one (or as many columns as were selected to the left of the selected ones).•
Delete•	At beginning or end of table: Select rows + at least one character outside the table, then press Delete. ¶ Within table: Select rows, press Control-Command-X.•	Select columns, then choose **Table Layout...** in **Format** menu, check *Column* and click *Delete*.•

BULLETS
Bullets inside cells mark end of text. When a bullet is not included in selection, text only is selected. When a bullet is included, text and cell are selected and can be cut/copied/put into Glossary, etc. Bullets at the right of rows are there so you can put the Insertion Point between the last cell and the bullet to add columns.

35

MENUS

There are three commands that give access to Word 5's Help program. The **About Microsoft Word...** command in the **Apple** menu, the **Help...** command in the **Window** menu and the **Microsoft Word Help...** command in the **Help** menu (this is the Balloon Help menu, which exists only with System 7).

If you don't find a topic through the alphabetical list of the Help program, there are other ways to look for it. See opposite page.

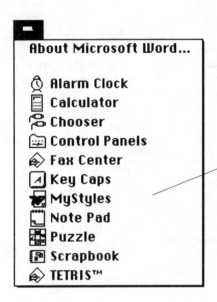

ALIAS

If you create a *Stationery* document with your favorite stylesheet (see p. 39) and if you have System 7, you might drag its alias to the **Apple** menu folder. It will then become an **Apple** menu command like *MyStyles* here. You may then use it to open new documents instead of choosing the **File** menu's **New** command.

TOPICS

When you choose an item in the list, a text about it replaces the list. The *Help* button is then replaced by a *Topics* button, which brings you back to the list.
The *Previous* and *Next* buttons display texts about the previous or next item.

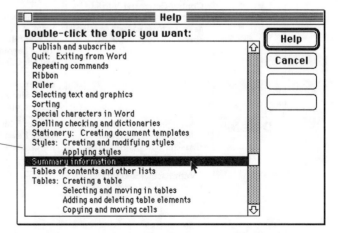

Pressing the Command and "?" keys is a traditional Macintosh shortcut for Help. On an extended keyboard, you can also press the Help key.

If you do this when a dialog box is open, the pertinent Help page is displayed immediately.

If no dialog box is open, the pointer becomes a fat question mark. Scrolling a menu and choosing a command with this question mark or clicking a part of the screen (e.g. the ribbon, or a paragraph, etc.) displays the pertinent Help page.

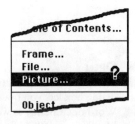

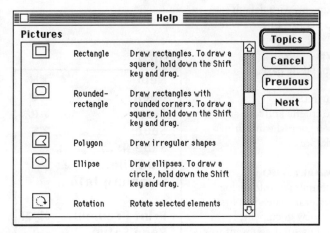

HELP POINTER
Choosing the **Picture...** command in the **Insert** menu with the *Help* Pointer as above displays the *Pictures* page of the Help program.

BALLOONS
The System 7 balloons work nicely with all the menu commands, dialog boxes and screen parts of Word 5.

37

MENUS

This is the default **File** menu when the screen is bigger than 9". The names of the four last opened documents (here, **Lincoln**, etc.) do not appear on a 9" menu, but a *Preferences* option lets you add the list if you wish (see p. 67).

All the menus also have hidden commands. Pressing Option-Command and the + or − sign of the alphabetic keyboard changes the Pointer into a fat **+** or **−** sign. See p. 84 for how to add commands with the **+** Pointer.

Choosing a command with the **−** Pointer removes it. You can remove **Lincoln** or **Einstein** in this way.

NEW
This opens an "untitled" document, with default settings defined in *Preferences*.

SAVE
See opposite page.

FIND FILE
Give criteria and find any file on your Macintosh/network. See p. 40.

SUMMARY INFO
The Summary Info dialog box appears when you first save a new document. Info is useful if you want to use *Find File* later. See p. 40.

PAGE SETUP, PRINT
See p. 42.

LINCOLN
Choosing one of these opens the document. A very convenient feature.

OPEN
The traditional Macintosh *Open* dialog box lets you open existing Word documents, as well as MacWrite II/Word for Windows/etc. documents if you have installed necessary "converters" (done by default in the standard installation).

CLOSE
When you are through with a document and want to open another one, do not go back to the Finder by quitting, but use **Close** and **Open...** commands.

PRINT PREVIEW
Word's most wysiwyg display mode. See p. 26 and 28.

MERGE
Form letters, etc. See p. 74.

File	
New	⌘N
Open...	⌘O
Close	⌘W
Save	⌘S
Save As...	
Find File...	
Summary Info...	
Print Preview...	⌘⌥I
Page Setup...	
Print...	⌘P
Print Merge...	
Lincoln	
Einstein	
Elvis	
Marilyn	
Quit	⌘Q

File: Save

If your three-year-old child pulls the plug for fun or if some unexpected glitch freezes the screen, the work you have done since the last time you saved to the hard disk is l-o-s-t.

Some books give clever advice, like, "*The three first Macintosh laws are Save, Save and Save.*" Most people ignore these laws until they lose two hours of work. Then they really save.

Word 5 is willing to prompt you, "Please save!" See p. 67.

The dialog box below is displayed the first time you save, or when you choose the **Save as...** command.

FOLDER
Pop-up menu lets you climb up the hierarchy of folders.

HARD DISK
Climb up hierarchy one step at a time by clicking this icon.

DESKTOP
Go to the Desktop to choose another volume, e.g. a floppy disk to back up your documents. Remembering to save is not enough, you must also remember to back up all documents.

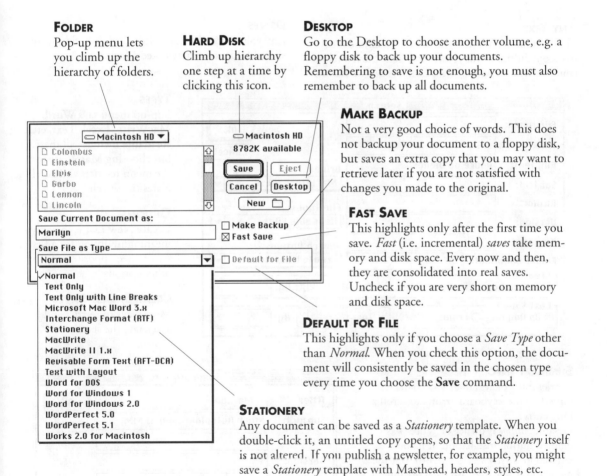

MAKE BACKUP
Not a very good choice of words. This does not backup your document to a floppy disk, but saves an extra copy that you may want to retrieve later if you are not satisfied with changes you made to the original.

FAST SAVE
This highlights only after the first time you save. *Fast* (i.e. incremental) *saves* take memory and disk space. Every now and then, they are consolidated into real saves. Uncheck if you are very short on memory and disk space.

DEFAULT FOR FILE
This highlights only if you choose a *Save Type* other than *Normal.* When you check this option, the document will consistently be saved in the chosen type every time you choose the **Save** command.

STATIONERY
Any document can be saved as a *Stationery* template. When you double-click it, an untitled copy opens, so that the *Stationery* itself is not altered. If you publish a newsletter, for example, you might save a *Stationery* template with Masthead, headers, styles, etc.

MENUS

This is a truly fantastic function. You might try it with a simple example like the one below. You should then be able to find many more ways to use it.

Although the command's name is **Find File...**, it opens a dialog box called *Search*, where you enter search criteria. The *Find File* dialog box, shown on the opposite page, appears as a result of a successful search and displays a list of files matching the criteria. Among possible criteria are the *Summary Info* data, which you enter when you save a new document for the first time.

ANY TEXT
In this example, Word 5 will search for all the files that contain the words *André de Dienes*. Such a name could be written with a "wild card": *Andr? de Dienes*.

DRIVES
Any volume can be examined; hard disk, floppy, or shared folder on a networked Macintosh

TYPES
Pop-up menu says **Word**, **MacWrite**, **Excel**, **Text**, etc. **Readable** includes all these, but choosing **MacWrite** in the menu restricts and accelerates the search.

OPTIONS
Create New List is the only meaningful option for a first search. See opposite page for other options.

CREATED, LAST SAVED
More ways to restrict and accelerate the search.

```
┌─────────────────── Search ───────────────────┐
│                                                │
│  File Name: [                    ]   ┌──────┐  │
│  Title:     [                    ]   │  OK  │  │
│                                      └──────┘  │
│  Any Text:  [André de Dienes    ]   ┌────────┐│
│  Subject:   [                    ]   │ Cancel ││
│  Author:    [                    ]   └────────┘│
│  Version:   [                    ]   Drives:    │
│  Keywords:  [                    ]   [Macintosh HD    ▼]│
│  Finder Comments: [           ]      File Types: │
│  ┌─Created──────────────────────┐   [Readable Files  ▼]│
│  │◉ On Any Day ○ From: 4/28/9 ⇕ To: 4/18/92 ⇕ By:[  ]│
│  ┌─Last Saved───────────────────┐  Search Options: │
│  │◉ On Any Day ○ From: 4/25/9 ⇕ To: 4/17/92 ⇕ By:[  ]│
│                                      [Create New List ▼]│
└────────────────────────────────────────────────┘
```

SUMMARY INFO
Entries must be less than 255 characters long. Use the keyboard arrows to scroll a long entry.

Default *Author* is owner of Word 5 as defined during installation or name entered in *Preferences* (see p. 66), but the name can be changed for each document.

```
┌═══════════════ Summary Info ═══════════════┐
│                                             │
│  Title:    [I, Marilyn              ]  ┌────┐│
│  Subject:  [Mock Autobiography of MM ] │ OK ││
│                                        └────┘│
│  Author:   [Greif                  ]  ┌──────┐│
│  Version:  [1                      ]  │Cancel││
│  Keywords: [Marilyn Monroe Norma Jean Bak]└──────┘│
└─────────────────────────────────────────────┘
```

40

The list of found documents below is rather short. When the list is longer, you can select several documents together by Shift-clicking, then you can open or print them together.

For example, if you are publishing a cinema newsletter and if you create one folder per issue, the *Find File* function will let you locate and open the articles about Marilyn Monroe across all the issues. To do this reasonably quickly, you should not use the *Any Text* box like in this example, but fill in *Summary Info* for each article you publish, then use the info as search criteria.

DIRECTORY
Pop-up menu gives you the path through the folder hierarchy for whatever file is selected in the list.

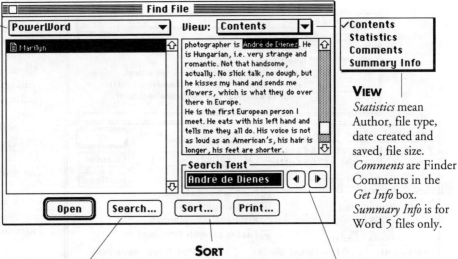

VIEW
Statistics mean Author, file type, date created and saved, file size. *Comments* are Finder Comments in the *Get Info* box. *Summary Info* is for Word 5 files only.

SEARCH
This button takes you back to the *Search* dialog box, where you can enter new criteria.
Now you can use the *Search Options*. If you choose **Create New List**, you begin a new search altogether. If you choose **Add Matches to List**, files matching the new criteria are added to the list (an *or* search; list has files matching one set of criteria *or* the other). If you choose **Search Only in List**, files not matching the new criteria are deleted from list (an *and* search; list has files matching the first *and* second set of criteria).

SORT
This sorts the files in the list according to the orders in the Finder's **View** menu; by Name, by Size, by Type, etc.

PREVIOUS, NEXT
These buttons take you to the next or previous occurence of the *Search Text* in the *Contents* view of the document.

41

MENUS

The traditional Macintosh dialog boxes shown below offer options for LaserWriter and StyleWriter printers. The ImageWriter page setup is a little different. See your printer's manual.

If your document does not include bitmap text (i.e., pre-TrueType Chicago), bitmap pictures (made with MacPaint or HyperCard) or PostScript effects (see p. 89), you can just accept these default settings.

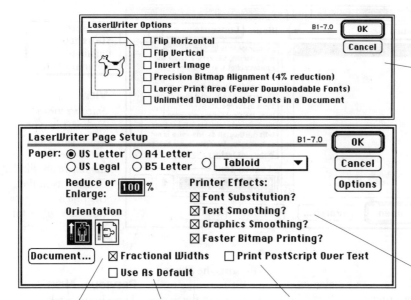

OPTIONS
The *Options* button opens this dialog box.
Try *Flip*, etc. and see what happens to the little dog.
Precision Bitmap Alignment is a must if you print unsmoothed bitmap pictures, e.g. screen captures.
Larger Print Area means 0.25" margin instead of 0.5".
Downloadable fonts are fonts like Garamond, which are not permanent residents of the LaserWriter's memory.

SMOOTHING
Text Smoothing affects pre-TrueType versions of fonts with city names. Bitmap pictures are printed with crisp edges and usually look better when Graphics Smoothing is turned off.

FRACTIONAL WIDTHS
Unchecking this option makes somes screen fonts easier to read, but you must not forget to check it again before printing if you want professional-looking type.

DEFAULT
Page Setup choices affect only the current document.
Check this box if you want these settings for all new documents.

POSTSCRIPT
By default, PostScript effects are printed in background, i.e. *under* text. Check this if you want them on top of text.

42

It is quite legitimate to be nervous when the paper version of the document comes out of the printer. Even if the printer works well and there is enough paper in the paper tray, unexpected things can (and will) happen. A title that should be at the top of a page has moved to the bottom of the preceding one, etc.

To be on the safe side, you should check your document carefully, before printing, in *Page Layout* view or *Print Preview*.

TAB

In Dialog boxes, you can send the Insertion Point from one little box to the next one by pressing the Tab key instead of clicking with the I-Beam Pointer.

For example, to print from p. 1 to 5, you would press Tab, type 1, press Tab, type 5, then press Return or Enter to print.

FROM

To print only p. 5, you should enter From: 5 To: 5.

COVER

A page with the document's name, printing time and other info, to be printed before or after the document.

```
LaserWriter  "Personal LaserWriter NT"         B1-7.0    [ Print  ]
Copies: [1]         Pages: ◉ All  ○ From: [    ]  To: [    ]  [ Cancel ]
Cover Page:    ◉ No ○ First Page  ○ Last Page
Paper Source: ◉ Paper Cassette   ○ Manual Feed
Print:         ○ Black & White   ◉ Color/Greyscale
Destination:   ◉ Printer         ○ PostScript® File
Section Range: From: 1    To: 1       ☐ Print Selection Only
☐ Print Hidden Text  ☐ Print Next File  ☐ Print Back To Front
```

COLOR/GREYSCALE

This option is not only for color and color printers, but also for documents with shades and pictures printed on a LaserWriter.

HIDDEN TEXT

A style of text which you can choose to print or not.

SECTION

If your document is divided in sections, you can print *All Pages* of sections 2 to 5, etc.

NEXT FILE

This box highlights if you have established *File Series* (see *Document* dialog box, p. 29).
You can also print several documents by selecting their icons on the Finder and using the Finder's print command or by using the *Find File* function (see p. 41).

SELECTION

This box highlights only when you have selected some text in your document.

MENUS

The **Edit** menu exists in most Macintosh programs. It always includes the basic and easy *Cut/Copy/Paste* functions, which are described on p. 12.

As *Publish/Subscribe*, a new System 7 technique, and other ways to link documents are a little less easy (but still invented by human beings for human beings), they are explained through examples on p. 76 to 82.

UNDO
Your last action can usually be undone. The command then remains highlighted and mentions the action.
When the command is dimmed, it means the action cannot be undone.

PASTE
When you Shift-scroll the menu, this command becomes **Paste Object** (see p. 78).

PASTE SPECIAL
Dialog box includes the *Paste Link* button, which creates links. Command becomes **Paste Link** when you Shift-scroll (see p. 76).

GO TO
Dialog box lets you enter a page number.

CREATE PUBLISHER
This command is highlighted only when some text is selected. See p. 80.

SUBSCRIBE TO
Open-type dialog box shows list of possible *Editions* you can subscribe to. See p. 80.

Edit	
Undo Typing	⌘Z
Repeat	⌘Y
Cut	⌘X
Copy	⌘C
Paste	⌘U
Paste Special...	
Clear	
Select All	⌘A
Find...	⌘F
Replace...	⌘H
Go To...	⌘G
Glossary...	⌘K
Create Publisher...	
Subscribe To...	
Link Options...	
Edit Object...	

REPEAT
Last action is mentioned when it can be repeated: **Repeat Typing**, etc. This is a very useful command. You can format characters/a paragraph, then apply the same formatting to other characters/paragraphs.

CLEAR
Pressing the Delete key is the usual way to Clear text.

SELECT ALL
You can also Command-click in the *Selection Bar* to **Select All** (see p. 11).

FIND/REPLACE
See opposite page.

GLOSSARY
See p. 32.

LINK OPTIONS
This command becomes **Object Options...**, **Subscriber Options...** or **Publisher Options...**, depending on element selected.

EDIT OBJECT
This command highlights when an *Embedded Object* is selected.

44

The basic purpose of this function is, for example, to replace *Peking* by *Beijing* throughout a book about China.

In Word 4, you could only replace text by text, but Word 5 also lets you find/replace formatted text. You can replace **Beijing** by *Beijing* or by BEIJING everywhere.

The example below shows the replacement of normal Garamond italicized with the Macintosh Italic style by the special *Garamond Italic* font. This would apply to any text in italicized Garamond, so the text boxes stay empty.

FORMAT
Pop-up menu lets you open format dialog boxes. You can also define format on ribbon and ruler. **Clear** deletes all the formatting displayed under the text box.

FIND NEXT
The *Find* dialog box is similar to the upper part of this one. You can't *Replace*, but you find the next occurence of what you're looking for.

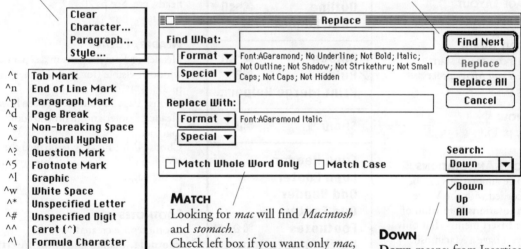

MATCH
Looking for *mac* will find *Macintosh* and *stomach*.
Check left box if you want only *mac*, *Mac* or *MAC*. Check right box if you don't want upper case in this example.

SPECIAL
Choosing a command in this pop-up menu enters the symbols shown left into the *Find What* text box. Commands in *Replace With* pop-up menu are slightly different.
You can write the symbols directly if you want, and enter other special characters as ^*n*, where *n* is an ASCII number, e.g. ^32 for space, etc. Numbers can be known through the **Symbol...** command of the **Insert** menu (see p. 52).

DOWN
Down means: from Insertion point to the end of the document, then from beginning to Insertion Point. **Up** means: the other way around. **All** means: From beginning to end.
If you select text before choosing **Find.../Replace...**, the *Down* option becomes **Selection**.

45

MENUS

This menu controls how you display the document and what parts of it you show.

Ribbon and Ruler are shown by default. In the default menu, there is only one **Header** (and one **Footer**) command.

Shown below is the menu for the Marilyn document, where the *Even/Odd Headers* option of the *Document* dialog box has been checked (see p. 29).

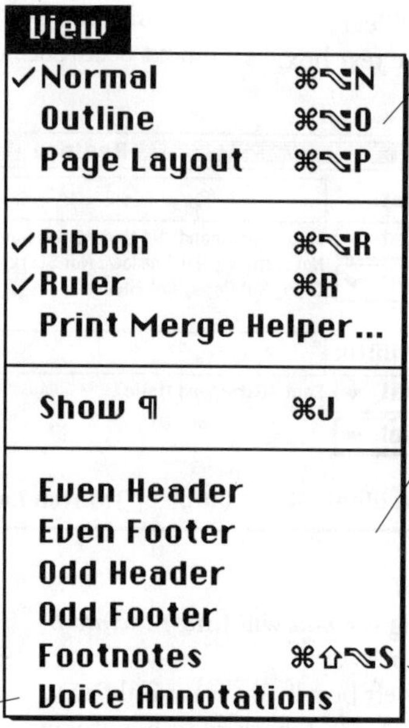

NORMAL
Default view is not wysi-wyg: text flows continuous-ly, with page breaks marked by dotted lines.

PAGE LAYOUT
See opposite page.

PRINT MERGE
This command starts the *Print Merge* process. See p. 74.

SHOW ¶
See p. 15.

VOICE ANNOTATIONS
Voice annotations can be recorded with the **Voice Annotations** command of the **Insert** menu – but only if you have a Macintosh with a microphone.
The voice annotations in a document are symbolized by small loudspeakers, and can be listened to, whether you have a microphone or not, by choosing this **Voice Annotations** command.
See p. 51.

```
View
✓ Normal              ⌘⌥N
  Outline             ⌘⌥O
  Page Layout         ⌘⌥P

✓ Ribbon              ⌘⌥R
✓ Ruler               ⌘R
  Print Merge Helper...

  Show ¶              ⌘J

  Even Header
  Even Footer
  Odd Header
  Odd Footer
  Footnotes           ⌘⇧⌥S
  Voice Annotations
```

OUTLINE
A very convenient way to build and modify a text with several hierarchical levels of titles, subtitles, paragraph heads, etc. See p. 70.

HEADER, FOOTER
Header or Footer opens in a separate window, visible (for Even Header) on p. 27.
Choose Page Layout view to see how Header, Footer and main text look together.
Choose Print Preview to change the position of Header and Footer relative to the page.

FOOTNOTES
Footnotes are created with the **Footnote...** command of the **Insert** menu.
They belong to a separate window, which you can open with this **Footnotes** command.
Double-clicking the footnote refer-ence mark also opens this window. See p. 50.

If you just write text that will be imported later into a DTP program, without Header, Footer and notes, you never need to switch to *Page Layout* view.

If your DTP program is Word 5, i.e. if you want your printed pages to look good, you certainly want to see Header, Footer, notes and text together on the page as they will appear when printed. This is done by choosing the **Page Layout** command.

In the example below, the *Normal* view of a three-column text (left) shows only one column. In the *Page Layout* view (right), you see three columns, Header and margins.

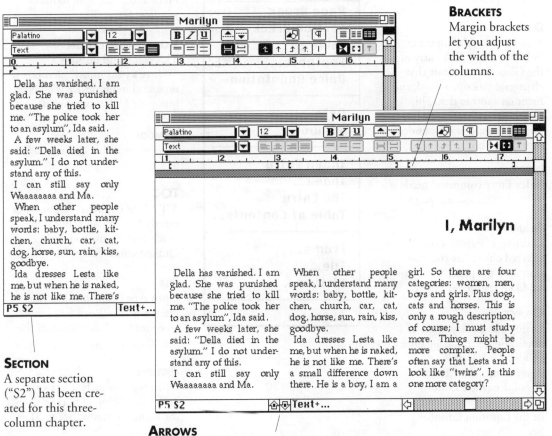

BRACKETS
Margin brackets let you adjust the width of the columns.

SECTION
A separate section ("S2") has been created for this three-column chapter.

ARROWS
Clicking arrows displays previous/next page.

MENUS

If you are a complete beginner, you may wait for a while before trying all the powerful commands of this menu. Most of them are not available in standard word processing programs like MacWrite II and WriteNow (the main exceptions are **Page Break** and **Footnote...**).

PAGE & SECTION BREAK
See opposite page.

TABLE
Opens the *Insert Table* dialog box. See p. 34.

DATE
This inserts at the Insertion Point the *Print Date* entry of the Glossary, i.e. a date that changes if you open the document on another day. This date is like a character; when *Show ¶* is on, it is surrounded by a dotted box.

INDEX
Index Entry command needs to be customized. See p. 53.

FRAME
Creating a "frame" around a selected object lets you position it on the page. A powerful DTP feature. See p. 82.

OBJECT
Dialog box displays a list of applications supporting OLE (*Object Linking and Embedding*), like Excel, Word, Equation Editor. This is where you open Excel or the Equation Editor. See p. 78 and 86.

Insert

Insert	
Page Break	⇧〜
Section Break	⌘〜
Table...	
Footnote...	⌘E
Voice Annotation	
Date	
Symbol...	
Index Entry	
Index...	
TOC Entry	
Table of Contents...	
Frame...	
File...	
Picture...	
Object...	

FOOTNOTE
Pressing Command-E and Enter fast enough bypasses the *Footnote* dialog box: an automatic footnote number appears at the Insertion Point and in the split footnote window. See p. 50.

VOICE ANNOTATION
This command displays a "Where's your mike?" alert box if no sound input device is plugged into your Macintosh. See p. 51.

SYMBOL
Displays available characters. See p. 52.

TOC
A Table of Contents can be made exactly like an index, but it makes much better sense to use the Outline mode. See p. 70.

FILE
Open type dialog box lets you insert a whole Word 5 or otherwise "readable" document at the Insertion Point.

PICTURE
Open type dialog box lets you insert an existing picture or display the Picture window. See p. 31.

Insert: Page Break

The left picture shows exactly what happens when you insert a *Page Break:* text after the break is sent to the top of the next page. This is a *Print Preview* picture. In *Normal* view, all you see is a dotted line in the middle of the text.

A *Section Break* appears in *Normal* view as a double dotted line. By default, a new section begins on the next page. You can format it to begin on the same page, as in the right picture below, in the *Section* dialog box (see p. 56).

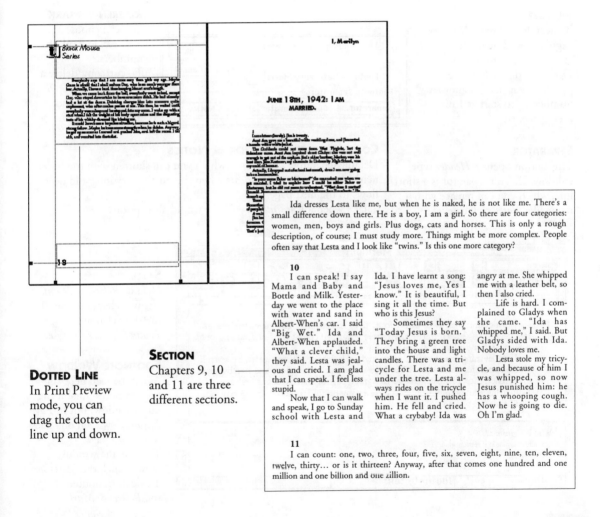

DOTTED LINE
In Print Preview mode, you can drag the dotted line up and down.

SECTION
Chapters 9, 10 and 11 are three different sections.

Ida dresses Lesta like me, but when he is naked, he is not like me. There's a small difference down there. He is a boy, I am a girl. So there are four categories: women, men, boys and girls. Plus dogs, cats and horses. This is only a rough description, of course; I must study more. Things might be more complex. People often say that Lesta and I look like "twins." Is this one more category?

10
I can speak! I say Mama and Baby and Bottle and Milk. Yesterday we went to the place with water and sand in it. Albert-When's car. I said "Big Wet." Ida and Albert-When applauded. "What a clever child," they said. Lesta was jealous and cried. I am glad that I can speak. I feel less stupid.

Now that I can walk and speak, I go to Sunday school with Lesta and Ida. I have learnt a song: "Jesus loves me, Yes I know." It is beautiful, I sing it all the time. But who is this Jesus?

Sometimes they say "Today Jesus is born." They bring a green tree into the house and light candles. There was a tricycle for Lesta and me under the tree. Lesta always rides on the tricycle when I want it. I pushed him. He fell and cried. What a crybaby! Ida was angry at me. She whipped me with a leather belt, so then I also cried.

Life is hard. I complained to Gladys when she came. "Ida has whipped me," I said. But Gladys sided with Ida. Nobody loves me.

Lesta stole my tricycle, and because of him I was whipped, so now Jesus punished him: he has a whooping cough. Now he is going to die. Oh I'm glad.

11
I can count: one, two, three, four, five, six, seven, eight, nine, ten, eleven, twelve, thirty… or is it thirteen? Anyway, after that comes one hundred and one million and one billion and one zillion.

49

MENUS

Standard *Footnote Reference Number*, *Footnote Separator* and *Footnote* can be seen in wysiwyg *Page Layout* view on p. 27.

In *Normal* view, footnotes are displayed inside a "split window." This is very convenient when the footnote reference mark is at the top of a page, as in the example below: unless you have a big screen, you could not see the reference and the footnote at the same time in *Page Layout* view.

NUMBER

By default, *Reference Numbers* begin at 1 and never stop growing. Options in the *Document* dialog box (see p. 29) let you start at another number, or re-start at 1 on every page, etc.

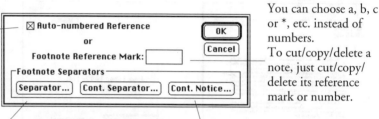

REFERENCE MARK

You can choose a, b, c or *, etc. instead of numbers.
To cut/copy/delete a note, just cut/copy/delete its reference mark or number.

SEPARATOR

This button opens a *Header* type window. Default separator is a short line, which you can replace with a name like *Notes*, or whatever.

CONTINUATION SEPARATOR & NOTICE

Default separator, a long line (which you can shorten with the Indent markers, replace, etc.), appears when the note is very long and overflows to the next page.
That's when a *Continuation Notice* would also appear.

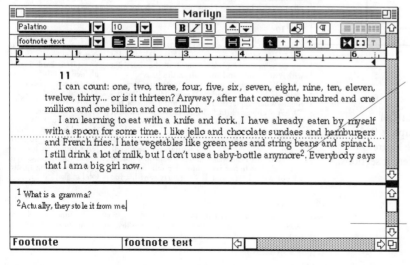

STYLE

Default *Reference Number* size was changed from 9 to 10 by changing *Footnote Reference* style.

FOOTNOTE WINDOW

As can be seen here, all the footnotes inhabit the same window, but in *Page Layout* view each one goes to its own page.
To close the window, double-click the *Split-Box*. To open it, double-click the *Reference Mark*.

Insert: Footnote, Voice A.

The first dialog box lets you record the sound. The **Voice Annotation** command of the **Insert** menu will display it only if your Macintosh has a microphone. When the recording is done and you click OK, a little loudspeaker symbol is pasted at the Insertion point.

The second dialog box appears when you select a loudspeaker symbol by dragging over it, then double-click it or choose the **Voice Annotations** command of the **View** menu. It lets you hear the different sounds included in your document.

RECORD

This function has its own menus. You can save a recording in various formats, copy and paste it, etc.

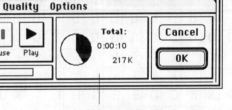

LOUDSPEAKER

Dotted underline means that this symbol is a "hidden character." Thus, if you want to use voice annotations in your documents, you should show hidden characters.
When this symbol is selected, you can cut and paste it to cut and paste a sound; save it to the Glossary, etc. An **Edit Voice Annotations...** command replaces **Edit Object...** in the **Edit** menu and opens the *Voice Record* dialog box, so that you can modify the sound.

TIME AND MEMORY

Recording can take enormous amounts of memory. **Options** let you put a time limit. **Quality** lets you choose a lower (compressed) quality.

PLAY

This dialog box lets you play the selected sound and navigate to other sounds.
Annotator initials are taken from the *Preferences* dialog box (see p. 66).

The clever **Symbol...** command replaces a very convoluted process: choosing the **Key Caps** command in the **Apple** menu, then selecting a font and pressing the Option key to locate that stupid é.

With the *Symbol* window, you just click é to insert it at the Insertion Point. The font shown in the window is the font at the Insertion point (below, Palatino), but you can choose another one in the **Font** menu.

By the way: *Symbol* is also the name of a Greek and mathematical characters font installed on most Macintosh computers. Pressing Shift-Command-Q switches the selected text or *one* character after the Insertion point to the *Symbol* font.

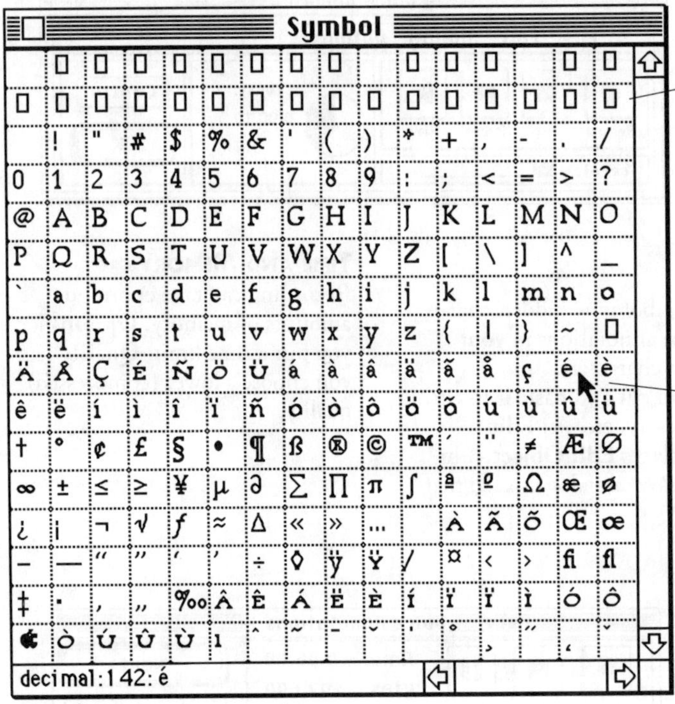

Symbol window

```
                                   ⬆
! " # $ % & ' ( ) * + , - . /
0 1 2 3 4 5 6 7 8 9 : ; < = > ?
@ A B C D E F G H I J K L M N O
P Q R S T U V W X Y Z [ \ ] ^ _
` a b c d e f g h i j k l m n o
p q r s t u v w x y z { | } ~ □
Ä Å Ç É Ñ Ö Ü á à â ä ã å ç é è
ê ë í ì î ï ñ ó ò ô ö õ ú ù û ü
† ° ¢ £ § • ¶ ß ® © ™ ´ ¨ ≠ Æ Ø
∞ ± ≤ ≥ ¥ µ ∂ ∑ ∏ π ∫ ª º Ω æ ø
¿ ¡ ¬ √ ƒ ≈ ∆ « » … À Ã Õ Œ œ
– — " " ' ' ÷ ◊ ÿ Ÿ / ¤ ‹ › fi fl
‡ · ‚ „ ‰ Â Ê Á Ë È Í Î Ï Ì Ó Ô
  Ò Ú Û Ù ı ˆ ˜ ¯ ˘ ˙ ˚ ¸ ˝ ˛ ˇ  ⬇
```

decimal: 1 42: é

The index at the end of this book was made with Word 5. Two separate steps are involved:

1. In the text of the document, mark the words to be indexed by selecting them and choosing the **Index Entry** command.

2. Compile (i.e., create) the index by choosing the **Index...** command and clicking *Start* in the dialog box below.

Word 5 puts the index at the end of the document, after a Section break.

INDEX ENTRY

Double-clicking a word to select it and choosing the **Index Entry** command puts hidden characters around the word to mark it as an index entry.

As this sequence of actions is to be repeated several hundred times, simplifying it is no luxury: see p. 84 for how to ascribe a keyboard shortcut to a command. In this example, the custom shortcut is Control-I. If you have an extended keyboard, you might prefer a function key.

By the way: .i.Symbol ;is also the name

SPACE

When you select a word by double-clicking, Word 5 includes the space following the word into the selection. The index will read Symbol 52 whether this space is included or not. The index format also ignores character and paragraph formatting in the original text (italics, etc.), but relies on the standard *Index* styles, which you may modify.

SUBENTRIES

Type a colon to create a Subentry. Entries ".i.Symbol:command;" and ".i.Symbol:font;" would appear in the index as:

Symbol
   command 52
   font 52

if Format was *Nested* (default), and as:

Symbol: command 52; font 52

if it was *Run-in*.

Other codes are .ib. for bold numbers, .ii. for italics, etc.

See the Word 5 manual for more.

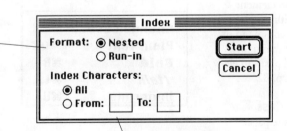

ALL CHARACTERS

If the index is to be very long, you can speed its creation by compiling, for example, first from A to M then from N to Z.

53

MENUS

If you are but one link in an editorial chain, and if some other people are going to import your text into a DTP program, you should be careful about formats.

The best policy might be not to format your text at all. Art directors in a magazine, for example, should circulate a sheet with precise rules for writers, like *Never Underline*, but they don't always do it…

CHARACTER
See opposite page.

SECTION
Dialog box lets you make choices for active Section. See p. 56. Reminder: New Section is created with **Section Break** command of **Insert** menu. See p. 49.

BORDER
Put borders around paragraphs, table cells, pictures. See p. 57.

FRAME
Position an element framed with the **Frame…** command of the **Insert** menu, or frame and position element. See p. 82.

CHANGE CASE
See opposite page.

Format	
Character...	⌘D
Paragraph...	⌘M
Section...	
Document...	
Border...	
Table Cells...	
Table Layout...	
Frame...	
Style...	⌘T
Revert To Style	⌘⇧↵
Change Case...	
✓Plain Text	⌘⇧Z
Bold	⌘B
Italic	⌘I
Underline	⌘U

PARAGRAPH
Apply formatting to active paragraph or selected paragraph(s). See p. 18.

DOCUMENT
Dialog box lets you define settings for whole document. See p. 29.

TABLE
Control shape of table created with **Table…** command of **Insert** menu. See p. 34.

STYLE
Dialog box lets you build and modify style sheet. See p. 24.

REVERT TO STYLE
Let's say you've changed the formatting of a *Text* style paragraph, so that its style reads *Text+*… This commands lets you re-format the paragraph to the original *Text* style.

BOLD, ETC.
These character formats are more easily applied with the buttons on the ribbon.
You might customize this menu and add other character styles here, like *Small Caps*, etc., which you can't choose on the ribbon. See p. 84.

54

This dialog box gives you more options than the ribbon.

Character formatting applies to selected characters and to new characters you'll type after the selection, or to new characters you'll type after the Insertion Point.

You may choose a color for text even if you have a black and white screen. The color will show if the document is transfered to a Macintosh with a colour monitor or printed on a color printer.

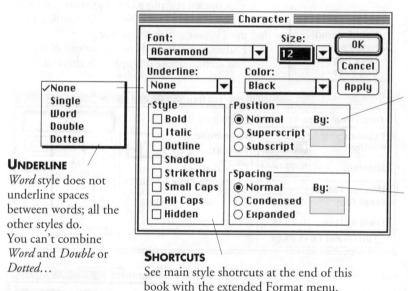

UNDERLINE
Word style does not underline spaces between words; all the other styles do.
You can't combine *Word* and *Double* or *Dotted*...

SHORTCUTS
See main style shotrcuts at the end of this book with the extended Format menu.

POSITION
See *Subscript* and *Superscript* examples on p. 15.
See a *Superscript by 15* text on p. 30.
Number in *By* box should be in pt. The program rounds a decimal number to the nearest integer.

SPACING
Default *Condensed* Spacing is by 1.5 pt. Number must belong to the 0.25 to 1.75 range, with 0.25 increments.
Default *Expanded* Spacing is by 3 pt. Number must belong to the 1 to 14 range, with 0.25 increments.

CHANGE CASE
Whereas *All Caps* (see above), a character Style, can be part of a Style Sheet, the options of this dialog box act like the Shift key: *Uppercase* stays *Uppercase* when you change style.

You create a section with the **Section Break** command of the **Insert** menu.

The double dotted line that seems to come before the beginning of a new section actually marks the end of the preceding one and "stores" its section settings. If you delete it, the preceding section takes the formatting of the new one. You can double-click the section mark to open the dialog box below.

You might divide a document into sections to create chapters, with different Headers/Footers, and Endnotes; or to change the number of columns somewhere, like in the p. 49 example.

NEW PAGE

This default option is the logical choice for a new chapter. You can also start a chapter on an even or odd page.

No Break means the section starts without a page break. This is the case in the p. 49 example.

You would choose **New Column** to put Endnotes at the end of a column, for example.

FIRST PAGE

When this box is checked, **First Header** and **First Footer** commands appear in the **View** menu so you can create a title page. The page number is hidden on a *First page*.

Note that this is completely different from a *Cover Page* (see p. 43).

ENDNOTES

This option is dimmed for regular notes: you need to choose *End of Section* for footnotes in the *Document* dialog Box (see p. 29).

Endnotes will be gathered at the end of the first section where this option is checked.

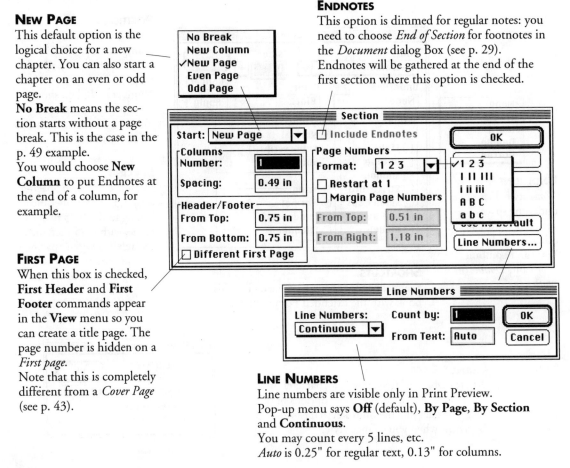

LINE NUMBERS

Line numbers are visible only in Print Preview.

Pop-up menu says **Off** (default), **By Page**, **By Section** and **Continuous**.

You may count every 5 lines, etc.

Auto is 0.25" for regular text, 0.13" for columns.

The *Border* or *Shading* you define in this dialog box applies to the active paragraph; the paragraphs you'll write after it will have the same kind of border or shading unless you change it.

You may also select paragraphs, cells in a table or pictures and define borders or shadings for them.

As it is a paragraph format, a border or shading can be part of a style (see example on p. 23). You can save it into a Glossary, and adjust its width by moving the Indent markers.

The Word 5 manual gives an interesting example of a gray bar created by shading an empty paragraph (see also p. 83).

CUSTOM BORDER

Clicking here and there in this box lets you put lines above or below paragraphs, to the right or left of them, or around and in-between them.

If you just want a border around a paragraph, click a Preset one.

FROM TEXT

Default distance between text and border is 2 pt. The number (from 1 to 31 pt) you enter here is added to this default distance.

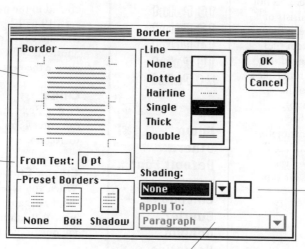

SHADING

The title box at the top of this page shows what a shaded paragraph looks like. The gray colour doesn't ressemble the screen pattern in the pop-up menu; its quality depends on the printer.

APPLY TO

This is dimmed unless several borders are possible. For example, if you select a picture, the pop-up menu says **Paragraph** and **Picture**, since you can put a border either around the picture or around the paragraph it is a part of.

For a table, the pop-up menu says **Paragraph**, **Selected Cells**, **Each Cell In Table**, **Entire Columns Selected** and **Entire Rows Selected**. The custom *Border* box then changes according to the choice you make in the pop-up menu, and the *Shadow* preset border is not available.

57

MENUS

The list of fonts in this menu depends on the System of your Macintosh. The Macintosh manuals explain how to add fonts to the System file.

There are several categories of fonts.

City-named, *Bitmap* fonts like Geneva or New York look more or less the same on the screen and when printed. You should avoid them when printing on a LaserWriter.

Outline fonts, like Helvetica, Times or Palatino print much better than they look on screen. Recent versions of Helvetica and Times are also *TrueType* fonts, which look good on screen whatever their size. More about this on the opposite page.

SCREEN FONT

As Palatino, chosen here, is not a *TrueType* font, it consists of two kinds of files: Screen files (dragged into the System file) and a Printer file (dragged into the System folder for fonts like Garamond; built-in to the LaserWriter for Palatino). Five screen files have been installed (out of six possible). Their numbers are "outlined" in the menu. For *TrueType* fonts, all the numbers are outlined.

DEFAULT FONT

See opposite page.

MT EXTRA

A special Equations font, automatically added to the System file when you install Word 5.

TTY & VT100

Special modem fonts, added to the System file when you install a modem.

Font

9 Point
10 Point
✓12 Point
14 Point
18 Point
24 Point

Up   ⌘]
Down   ⌘[
Other...
Default Font...

Chicago
Courier
Geneva
Helvetica
Monaco
MT Extra
New York
✓Palatino
Symbol
Times
TTYFont
VT100

UP & DOWN

These commands let you choose sizes not offered in the menu. For example, you can get a 19 or 17 pt font by selecting 18 pt text and choosing Up or Down. Shortcuts Shift-Command-> and < let you choose the next *menu* size.

OTHER

Dialog Box requests a size number. You can enter 19 or 17, or any number from 4 to 16,383.

CH FOR CHICAGO

When you type Shift-Command-E, the word *Font* appears in the Page Number area. You can then choose a font by entering one or two letters of its name.

LASERWRITER

Palatino is one of the LaserWriter's permanent fonts. The others are Avant Garde, Bookman, Courier, Helvetica, Helvetica Narrow, New Century Schoolbook, Times, Symbol, Zapf Chancery and Zapf Dingbats.

A floppy with the screen files for these fonts is included in the LaserWriter package. You don't need to install Printer files.

58

Font

The way the Macintosh handles fonts makes it very easy to play around with them. Art directors do not recommend it. You should try to adopt two main fonts: one for text and one for titles. For example, one *Serif* font, like Times or Palatino, for text, and one *Sans Serif* font, like Helvetica, for titles.

This book uses only one *Serif* font, Garamond, for text, and one *Sans Serif* font, Futura, for titles.

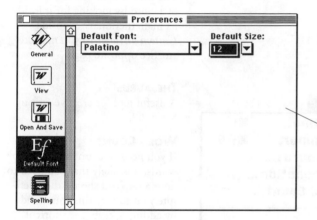

DEFAULT FONT

Choosing the **Default Font...** command opens this Preferences dialog box. The default font will replace New York for all new documents.

Do not adopt some exotic font, like Bodoni or Rockwell, if your document is to be transfered to another Macintosh: people who do not have the same font might find your text hard to read.

DISPLAY AND PRINT

The first line shows what happens for the LaserWriter fonts and some others (this one is Palatino 48): a size does not display well when the screen file for this size is not installed (left picture); it nevertheless prints OK (right picture).

The second line shows an "Adobe Type 1" font (Garamond). It is enough to install two screen sizes, like 10 and 12, if the System folder includes the program ATM (Adobe Type Manager). All sizes are then displayed OK.

The third line shows a TrueType font (Times). There is only one file, and the display is fine whatever the size.

MENUS

If you have installed all the dictionaries, the computer will check the spelling, grammar and style of your document, will hyphenate and count the words, but won't do the writing… yet.

The **Preferences…** command lets you customize your copy of Word 5 by choosing among several options, as is usually possible for most Macintosh programs. **Commands…** is much more powerful: you can revamp the application completely.

SPELLING
The program checks the spelling of a word by looking for it inside its main dictionary or inside *Custom dictionaries* you may create. See opposite page.

GRAMMAR
This function actually checks spelling at the same time as grammar and style. See p. 62.

HYPHENATION
You may have worked with programs where hyphenation is automatic. In Word, hyphenation is on demand. See p. 63.

SORT
Select paragraphs, or cells in a table, or a Tab-defined column (by Option-dragging), then choose this command to sort them in the ascending order of letters and numbers.
Press the Shift key when you scroll the menu to sort in descending order.

REPAGINATE NOW
When you've edited some text, Word 5 re-calculates page breaks and page numbers as soon as you pause. If you feel this *Background Repagination* slows things down, you can turn it off in *Preferences* (see p. 66), then *Repaginate* on demand with this command.

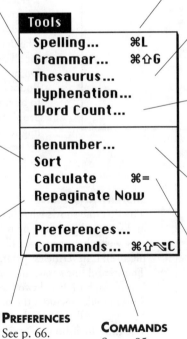

THESAURUS
A useful tool for creative writing. See p. 62.

WORD COUNT
If you need to count characters or words, it is likely that you need to do it a lot. You should then definitely customize this command by adding a keyboard shortcut here. See p. 84.

RENUMBER
This lets you number paragraphs. See p. 72.

CALCULATE
Select numbers in a table row or column, or in a tab-defined column, then choose this command to add them. The result is displayed in the *Page Number* area and copied to the Clipboard. You can also write a formula like (2+3)*4, select it and choose the command to calculate it.

PREFERENCES
See p. 66.

COMMANDS
See p. 85.

60

There are two ways you might use the main dictionary:

1. Check your document from beginning to end (this is also called *proofing*). A long and possibly tedious process, which you can improve by using the existing (empty at first) *Custom dictionary* or by creating new ones.

2. Select a word when you have some doubts about it and check its spelling without proofing the whole document.

1ST

This is typical of computer dictionaries: they usually find fault with your first word or so.

IGNORE

The spelling tool stops at every Waah, Gladys, Normadjin, etc. Leave the Pointer over this button, or your finger over the Enter key, to accept these words quickly.

IGNORE ALL

Click this button the first time the program stops at Gladys; then it won't stop anymore.

CHANGE ALL

When a suggestion meets your agreement, click this button to replace the wrong spelling by the right one throughout the document.

CUSTOM DICTIONARY

Clicking *Options...* displays the *Preferences* dialog box; checkmark dictionaries you want to open, or use the *Open...* button for dictionaries in other folders.

Open *Custom dictionaries* appear after *Add Words To* and in the pop-up menu. Clicking the *Add* button adds the unknown word to the chosen *Custom dictionary*. If none is open, you are asked to open one.

NEW DICTIONARY

Ignore All is a good way to skip Gladys, etc., during one proofing session. Creating a custom *Marilyn* dictionary also lets you validate such words for future sessions. Click *New...* to create and name a *Custom dictionary*.

The *Edit* button lets you remove words from the selected *Custom dictionary*.

ALWAYS SUGGEST

Unchecking this box speeds things. The *Suggest* button in the dialog box then becomes highlighted, so you can still get a suggestion on demand.

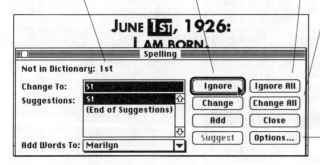

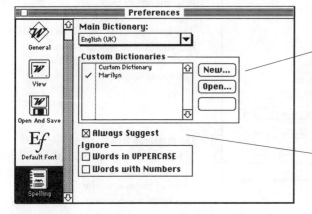

61

MENUS

One obvious thing you can do with the Grammar checker is to call your friends and show them how clever Mr Computer has become. Well, not that clever, actually: see the example below.

Despite such occasional failures, the Grammar checker can be a very useful tool. It does find mistakes which the Spelling checker has missed, and gives sensible (though very repetitive) advice on style.

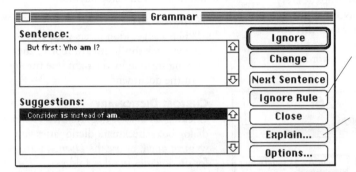

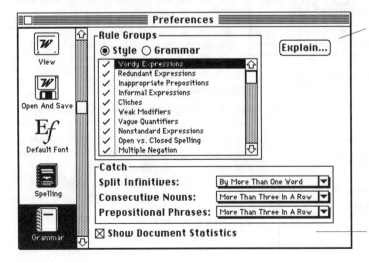

IGNORE RULE
This turns off a rule for the rest of the checking session. To ignore a rule altogether, turn it off in *Preferences*.

EXPLAIN
This explains a rule, often at great length, and gives examples. Schools should try this kind of software...

OPTIONS
The *Options...* button opens the *Preferences* dialog box, where you can decide (after testing them by trial and error) which style and grammar rules you want your document to be checked against.
The last option of the *Grammar* list lets you choose whether you want spelling checked as part of the Grammar checking.

DOCUMENT STATISTICS
When this box is checked (default option), Document Statistics are given at the end of the Grammar checking. See opposite page.

Tools: Grammar

The *Statistics* displayed after a Grammar check become significant only when there are enough sentences to feed them. If you need the *Statistics* but do not want to spend hours checking grammar, turn off all the rules before starting the check.

If all you need is the *Counts* part of the *Statistics*, you may skip the grammar check altogether by choosing the **Word Count...** command.

GRADES

The *Marilyn* story is aimed at people who are learning English. So it has short words, sentences and paragraphs. It rates very high ("Easy") on the 0-100 *Reading Ease* scale, and can be read by a person with a sixth or seventh grade education ("Fairly easy"). This book is rated seventh-eighth grade, i.e. average.

If you want your text to be rated "Difficult" or "Higher Education," use long words and sentences!

Document Statistics	
Counts:	
Words	13118
Characters	68254
Paragraphs	338
Sentences	1089
Averages:	
Sentences per Paragraph	3
Words per Sentence	12
Characters per Word	4
Readability:	
Passive Sentences	4%
Flesch Reading Ease	84.8
Flesch Grade Level	6.5
Flesch-Kincaid	4.2
Gunning Fog Index	6.3

OK

WORD COUNT

When you choose the **Word Count...** command, this dialog box opens and gives only a character count. This is a better character count than the one displayed in the Page Number area every time you save, since it applies either to the whole document or to selected text.

If you want other items to be counted, check their box and click the *Count* button.

Word Count	Main Text	Footnotes	Total
☒ Characters	68292	24	68316
☒ Words	13194	4	13198
☒ Lines	1281	2	1283
☒ Paragraphs	424	2	426

[Count] [Cancel]

63

MENUS

By default, the *Thesaurus* tool looks up the word that includes the Insertion Point, but it will also look up any word you enter into the *With* box.

When the initial word is *Gladys*, you don't get *Meanings* in the left box, but an alphabetical list with Give and Glad, etc.

The author of this book shares an opinion found in MacWorld magazine: this thesaurus is a mediocre one. Word Finder, by Microlytics (which used to be bundled with Word 4) is much better. It costs $70 or so.

MEANINGS
Selecting a word on this side displays a list of synonyms on the other side.

PUN
When you select *Related Words* for *Punish*, the list you get contains one word: *Pun*. Is this a joke?

LOOK UP
Selecting a word on this side and clicking Look Up moves the search ahead.

PATH
Pop-up menu shows the path followed from the Original word to the latest synonym. In this case: Punish Smite Lambaste Hurt Torment.

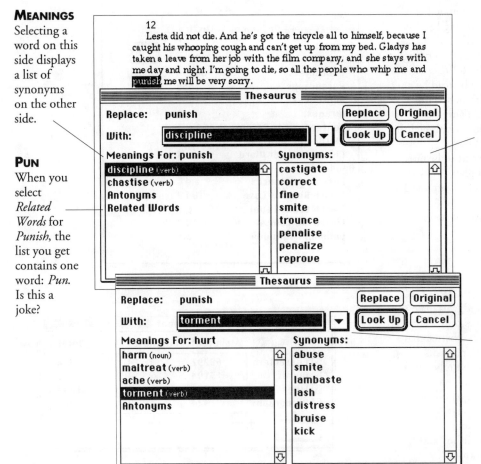

Tools: Thesaur., Hyphen.

Word's one-shot hyphenation cuts words that need hyphens here and now. As soon as you modify the document, new words need to be cut, and you should start the hyphenation process again. Thus, it is recommended to do it at the last possible moment (e.g. before printing).

More good advice from the Black Mouse: You might forget about hyphenation, except for narrow justified columns.

HYPHENATION
When you open the dialog box, the leftmost button says Start Hyphenation. Clicking it starts a word-by-word hyphenation process, in which you can control where the words are split.

In most cases, you'd probably prefer to click *Hyphenate All* (or *Hyphenate Selection,* if text has been selected) and be done with it!

MARGIN
Dotted vertical bar shows where the right margin might be.

Hyphenation

Hyphenate: or|ange

☐ **Hyphenate Capitalized Words**

[No Change]   [Change]   [Hyphenate All]   [Cancel]

It is nice to be sick. Your mother stays with you and makes fresh orange juice and tells you stories and offers you gifts. Albert-When also offered me a gift: a black and white dog who followed him in the street. I call it Tippy and play with it on my bed. He has a gooey tongue.

It is nice to be sick. Your mother stays with you and makes fresh orange juice and tells you stories and offers you gifts. Albert-When also offered me a gift: a black and white dog who followed him in the street. I call it Tippy and play with it on my bed. He has a gooey tongue.

It is nice to be sick. Your mother stays with you and makes fresh orange juice and tells you stories and offers you gifts. Albert-When also offered me a gift: a black and white dog who followed him in the street. I call it Tippy and play with it on my bed. He has a gooey tongue.

NO HYPHENATION
This is the original narrow justified column. Big gaps in third line. Program shows what it is willing to do.

DEFAULT
Done! You get this either when you click *Change* in the word-by-word process, or when you let the program *Hyphenate All.*

CUSTOM
The dotted Margin line tells you that *oran-* might jump up to line 3. This may not be absolutely lawful, but in narrow column situations you have no choice but to be bold.

To set this custom hyphen, just move the Insertion Point between *oran* and *ge* in the dialog box, and click *Change.* Notice that *stories* is cut as a consequence.

65

MENUS

The *Preferences* choices you make are saved into a file called "Word Settings (5)," located in the System folder (inside the *Preferences* folder for System 7). The *Commands* dialog box (see p. 85) lets you create several such files, if you want different *Preferences* settings for different situations.

Click an icon at the left of the dialog box to choose which set of preferences to display at right. See p. 59 for *Default Font*, p. 61 for *Spelling*, and p. 62 for *Grammar*.

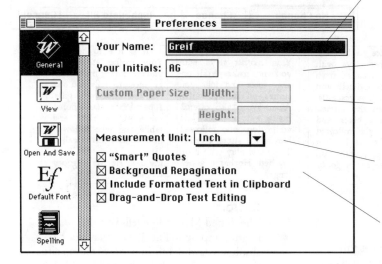

NAME
Default name is the one entered at installation time.
Changing the name here doesn't change the installation name, but rather the default *Author* name in *Summary Info* dialog boxes (see p. 40) and in the Glossary.

INITIALS
See Voice Annotations, p. 51.

CUSTOM PAPER
This highlights when the printer is an ImageWriter.

UNIT
Inches, centimeters, points or picas for ruler and dialog boxes.

SMART QUOTES, ETC.
Dumb quotes: ' and ".
Smart quotes: '...'and "...".
Background Repagination updates page breaks and number at idle time.
See Clipboard with formatted text on p. 12, Drag-and-Drop Text Editing on p. 13.

Tools: Preferences

Preferences' golden rule for lazy users: keep the default choices unless you know why you want to change them.

Remember that any change you make does not affect only the active document, but also all the Word 5 documents you'll open until you tinker with Preferences again.

OPEN AND SAVE

RTF is the Microsoft norm for text formatting.

Save Reminder doesn't save: it displays the alert box below.

VIEW

Picture Placeholders are gray rectangles that replace pictures for faster scrolling (but pictures still print).

Function Keys shortcuts are useful if you have an extended keyboard.

Short Menu Names are Int for Insert, Fmt for Format and Wnd for Window.

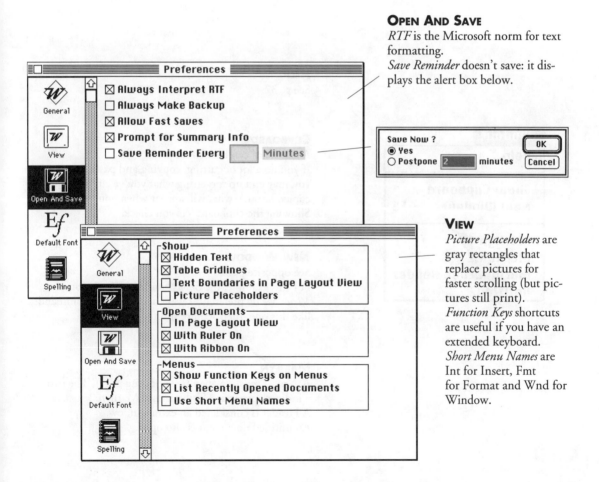

67

MENUS

You can open more than twenty documents or windows at the same time – if your computer has enough memory. The usual way to activate a visible window is to click it; if it is completely hidden behind another one, you can still activate it by choosing its name at the bottom of the Window menu.

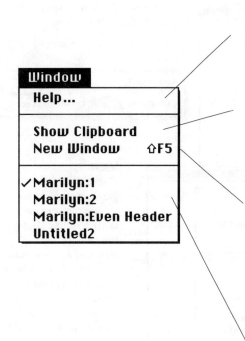

HELP
See p. 37.

CLIPBOARD
A clipboard can be seen on p. 12.
If you do a lot of cutting, copying and pasting, you may end up forgetting what you've cut or copied last, i.e. what will appear when you paste. Showing the clipboard lets you check.

NEW WINDOW
See opposite page.
For this example, the *Show Function Keys* option of *View: Menus* preferences was checked; some commands, like this one, then acquire shortcuts.

MARILYN
A *New Window* is open (see opposite page). The two windows appear as Marilyn:1 and Marilyn:2.
A Header is considered an extra window.
An untitled document is also open.

68

Split windows (shown on p. 22 and 50) let you see two parts of your document at the same time. You split and "un-split" a window by double-clicking or dragging the split-box. You may choose different *Views* for the two parts.

The **New Window** command also lets you see your document several times, but offers more possibilities. You can open more than two windows, and they are not stuck to each other like the two parts of a split window: you can move and resize them.

For example, if you have a big screen, you might keep a window with the outline of your document in a corner somewhere.

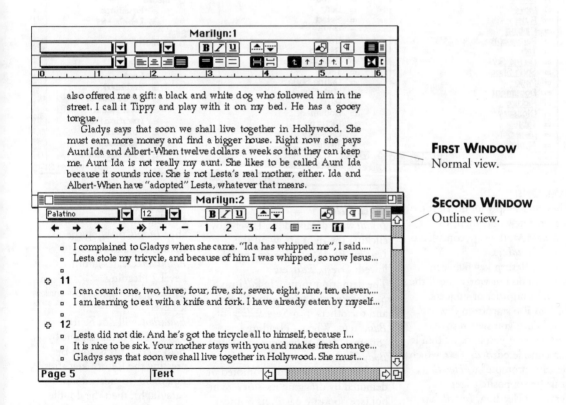

FIRST WINDOW
Normal view.

SECOND WINDOW
Outline view.

EXAMPLES

The document below seems to contain the beginning of this book, but in fact it is a special document created for this example. Its author being much too lazy to go through the outlining process, this book was not outlined but fully improvised!

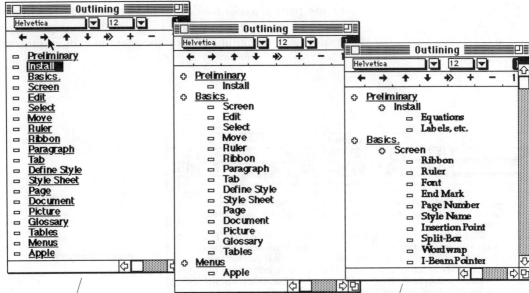

LEVEL ONE

When you simply jot down some ideas in a new document in *Outline* view, they are considered *Level 1 Headings*.
Press the Return key between ideas, but do not worry about the hierarchy or order of subjects. You can also start from *Normal* view. When you switch to *Outline*, what you have written is then considered *Body Text*, which you can "promote" to *Heading* status (see opposite page).
Here, one Heading, *Install*, has been selected.

LEVEL TWO

Install was "demoted" to Level 2 by clicking the right arrow on the *Outline Bar*. More demotions followed: *Screen*, *Edit*, etc.
The demotion turned *Install* into a *Subheading* of *Preliminary*, *Screen* and the others into *Subheadings* of *Basics*, etc. When a Heading has "Subtext" (i.e. *Subheadings* and/or *Body Text*), its – symbol turns into +. If a Heading is moved, promoted or demoted by dragging its + or – symbol (see opposite page), its Subtext moves with it.

LEVEL THREE

Moving the Insertion Point after *Install*, pressing the Return key and typing *Equations* creates another Level 2 Heading.
Clicking the right arrow makes it Level 3.
Equations will not be followed by Level 4 Headings, but by *Body Text*. This is done by pressing the Return key after *Equations* (to create a new paragraph), then the double arrow (to set the style of this paragraph to *Body Text*).

There are nine possible Levels for Headings, each with its own style. If you don't like the default styles, you can change them. At each level, Headings can be followed by Body Text.

When you select an *expanded* Heading by dragging over it or by clicking in the margin with the Pointer, its Body Text is selected with it and will move with it, but not its Subheadings.

If you select an expanded Heading by clicking its symbol, or a *collapsed* Heading by any means, its whole subtext is selected and will move with it.

LEFT
Promote Body Text to Heading. Promote Heading one level. Shortcuts – Drag symbol left. Press Option and Left keyboard arrow.

RIGHT
Demote Heading one level. Shortcuts – Drag symbol right. Press Option and Right keyboard arrow.

EXPAND/COLLAPSE
When a Heading is active (i.e. includes the Insertion Point) or selected alone, every click on + or – (shortcut: numeric keypad + or –) expands or collapses, that is shows or hides, one more level of Subtext. When Heading and Subtext are selected, a click (shortcut: double-click on symbol) expands or collapses all Subtext. Collapsed Subtext is symbolized by a dotted underline (see next page).

DISPLAY LEVELS
Click 1 to display only Level 1 Headings, click 2 to display Level 1 and Level 2, etc. When lower levels are hidden, it becomes much easier to organize the outline of a long document.

FIRST LINE
Show whole Body Text or just first line of paragraphs. Shortcut: Shift-Option-Down keyboard arrow.

TABS
Levels are aligned on default Tab stops. *Document* dialog box (see p. 29) lets you change 0.5" interval.

UP/DOWN
Move Heading above previous one/below next one. Shortcuts – Drag symbol up/down. Option–Up/Down keyboard arrow.

BODY TEXT
Convert a Heading to Body Text.

EXPAND ALL
Expand or collapse the whole outline. Shortcut: Numeric pad *.

FORMATTING
Display all Headings in Normal style or in *Headings* Styles.

71

EXAMPLES

The picture below shows a later stage of the outlining process. The document now includes Level 1, 2 and 3 Headings.

The Body Text can be written directly in Outline view, but if you prefer to see the structure of your document while you write, you should try splitting the screen or opening a new window. One part of the screen might show a semi-collapsed Outline like the one below, and you would write in *Normal* view in the other part of the screen.

NO SUBTEXT
The – symbol means that *Table of Contents* has no subtext yet.

COLLAPSED
Install, Screen and the other Level 2 Headings are followed by Body text, Level 3 Subheadings and more Body Text. All this is collapsed so that the structure of the document can appear.
Collapsed Subtext is symbolized by a dotted underline.

BODY TEXT
The *Paragraph* Heading is fully expanded, but only the first lines of Body Text are shown.

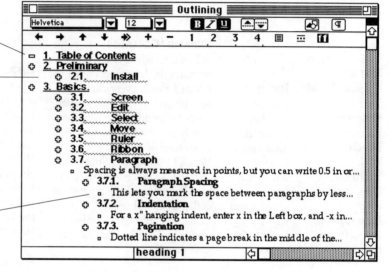

RENUMBER
Visible Headings can be numbered, as above. If the Outline starts with Body Text, visible Body Text paragraphs will also be numbered.
The default numbering format uses numbers and starts at 1 for every new level: *Basics* would be 3, *Screen* would be 1, *Edit* would be 2, etc. Shown above is the 1.1 format with numbers.
For example, write I.A.1.a.i in the *Format* box and check 1 if you want Basics to be III and Screen to be A; check 1.1 if you want Screen to be III.A.

BY EXAMPLE
You can number some Headings with your own scheme, then check this option to number the rest.

ALREADY
If you don't want a Heading (e.g. *Table of Contents*, above) to be numbered, delete its number, then order a new numbering after checking this option.

Outline: Renumber, TOC

When you start a document with an Outline, creating a Table of Contents becomes very easy: just choose the **Table of Contents...** command of the **Insert** menu, then tell the program which levels of Headings to retain.

If you need to create a Table of Contents for some improvised document, building a temporary Outline is much easier than inserting TOC entries (as in the *Index* process described on p. 53): switch to *Outline* view, then promote to Headings whatever titles you want in your Table of Contents.

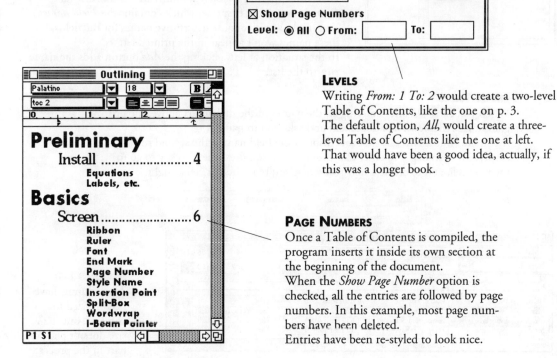

LEVELS

Writing *From: 1 To: 2* would create a two-level Table of Contents, like the one on p. 3.
The default option, *All,* would create a three-level Table of Contents like the one at left.
That would have been a good idea, actually, if this was a longer book.

PAGE NUMBERS

Once a Table of Contents is compiled, the program inserts it inside its own section at the beginning of the document.
When the *Show Page Number* option is checked, all the entries are followed by page numbers. In this example, most page numbers have been deleted.
Entries have been re-styled to look nice.

EXAMPLES

The Merge feature involves two types of documents. The *Main Document* is often a letter, as in this example. The *Data Document* is often a mailing list; one item in the list, i.e. one name + address, is called a *Record*. You write the letter only once. The program then prints one letter per Record.

As with other advanced features of Word, it is easy to implement and remember if you practice once a week, less so if you need it twice a year. This is where the **Print Merge Helper...** command in the **View** menu becomes quite handy.

BUILD DATA DOCUMENT

To begin the process, open or create the *Main Document*, i.e. a regular Word document, and put the Insertion Point at the very top of the page.

Choose the **Print Merge Helper...** command. *New Open*-type Dialog box says *Choose or Create a Data Document*. A *New* button opens the dialog box at left.

Data will appear as a table. Columns are *Fields*. Rows are *Records*, except the first one, which contains the *Field names*. You might as well choose descriptive names for the fields, but these names won't appear in the printed letters.

In the situation at left, clicking the *Add* button adds the name *city* to the list.

EMPTY TABLE

When you click *OK* after entering all the names in the dialog box above, the program opens the new Data document and asks you to name it.

It contains this table. The first row displays the field names, the second row is empty. You can begin to enter names and addresses. Press the Tab key to go to the next cell, and to create a new row when you're in the last cell at right.

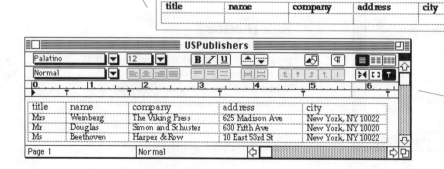

MAILING LIST

The columns have been resized for comfort, but their size doesn't play any part in the process.

Merge

If you do merge letters and data once a week, you may want to tinker with the *Print Merge Helper* function or bypass it altogether. You should know that the Data document table can be replaced by tab-separated field names and data. Similarly, to place a field name between double angle brackets in the Main document, simply type the name and use Option-\ for « and Shift-Option-\ for ».

INSERT FIELD NAME
When you click the *OK* button in the *Data Document Builder* dialog box, the *Helper bar* appears in the Main document. A pop-up menu offers field names. Choose a name to paste it between double angle brackets at the Insertion Point.
The Merge process will replace the field name by the contents of the field.

DATA
References to the Data document are inserted by the *Helper* function.
If you do it yourself: «DATA USPublishers» is enough when the two documents belong to the same folder.

DATE
This *Print Date* was entered with the **Date** command of the **Insert** menu (see p. 48).

KEYWORD
You might write: We are looking for «IF city="Tokyo"» a Japanese «ELSE»an American «ENDIF» partner.
Special Merge instructions or keywords IF, SET, ASK, INCLUDE are explained in the Word 5 manual.
See also: separate document for field names, using the Merge function to print labels, etc. 72 pages about Merge!

ERRORS
Click this button to check for missing », etc.

TO FILE
This button puts all the letters, separated by section breaks, into a new document named *Merge 1*, which you may edit and print.

PRINT MERGE
This button prints all the letters directly.
To print only some of the letters choose the **Print Merge...** command in the **File** menu; this lets you print *from Record a to Record b.*

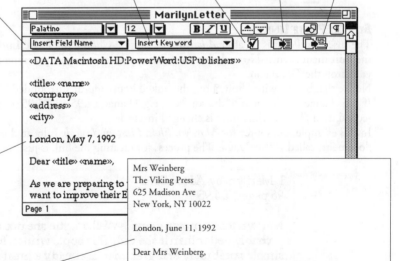

LETTER 1
This is the first letter, using the first record of the Data document.

75

EXAMPLES

Three linking techniques will be explained in the following pages. Another technique, *QuickSwitch*, which works with System 6 but not with System 7, is described in an annex of the Word 5 manual.

Technique #1 lets you link information inside a Word document, between two Word documents on the same hard disk, or between a Word and an Excel document on the same disk.

STEP 1: COPY INFO

The price that will appear after *A bargain at* in this catalog is to be linked to the price already written above. Step 1: Select and copy the price.

I, Marilyn, by Adam Greif
96 pages, £4.95

Marilyn tells her own story... Well, maybe she doesn't tell it herself, but it is probably better than if she did. This book, written for foreigners, with very simple vocabulary and grammar, is already a great success in Hungary and China. A bargain at

STEP 2: PASTE LINK

The Insertion Point is set after *A bargain at*. Step 2: Choose the **Paste Link** command in the **Edit** menu. Oh… No such command? But yes, there is: just press the Shift key while you scroll the *Edit* menu.

Notice that below, with Show ¶ on, the linked items appear surrounded by brackets.

If you change the first item ("the source"), e.g. change £4.95 to £ 5.95, or to $11.95, the second item ("the destination") is changed instantly.

In this example, the source for *Marilyn, Elvis, Einstein, Lincoln* is located in another Word document, called *#BlackMouse*. The process for creating the link is just the same.

I, Marilyn, by Adam Greif¶
96 pages, £4.95¶
¶
Marilyn tells her own story... Well, maybe she doesn't tell it herself, but it is probably better than if she did. This book, written for foreigners, with very simple vocabulary and grammar, is already a great success in Hungary and China. A bargain at £4.95¶
¶
Black Mouse mock biographies: Marilyn, Elvis, Einstein, Lincoln¶ ¶

You can *Paste Link* a picture inside Word. When you change the size or formatting of the source (inasmuch as Word 5 allows it), the destination is changed. You can also *Paste Link* text between Excel and Word 5.

With *QuickSwitch*, you could *Paste Link* a picture between its application and Word, or a table/chart between Excel and Word. When you edited the source, the destination was changed. This is now done with the *Object Embedding* feature (see next page), or with System 7's *Publish/Subscribe* function (see p. 80).

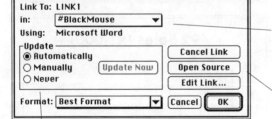

PASTE SPECIAL

The process described on the left page, via the **Paste Link** command, retains the "best" format, considering the source.

The **Paste Special...** command of the **Edit** menu adds one more step by displaying this dialog box; you may choose another format before Paste Linking, e.g. paste text without its formatting, or text as picture. *Word Document* pastes text as *Embedded Object*.

SOURCE OPTIONS

Selecting the source and choosing the **Link Options...** command in the **Edit** menu offers, well... one option: this is where you *Unlink*. You should *Unlink* (and *Cancel link*, below) before throwing away a linked document.

DESTINATION OPTIONS

Select the Destination and choose the **Link Options...** command to open this dialog box.

PATH

The pop-up menu shows the folder "path" to the source. If you move source or destination, you should *Edit Link* to update the path.

OPEN SOURCE

You click this button when the source belongs to a separate document and you want to edit it.

UPDATE

Default update of destination is automatic. Choosing *Manually* lets you control updates; also, you may then edit the destination – although any editing is lost when you update.

EXAMPLES

Possible *Embedded objects* are mostly Excel tables and charts; also, sounds and equations (see p. 86).

Embedding doesn't link two pieces of info like the preceding technique. There is only one item, inside one Word 5 document, but this item can be an Excel table or chart. When you double-click the object, Word 5 opens an Excel window where you can edit it. The link is between your document and the Excel *application*, which should be located on your hard disk.

In the example below, the object is initially imported from Excel. You can also create a new Excel object directly inside Word 5: see opposite page.

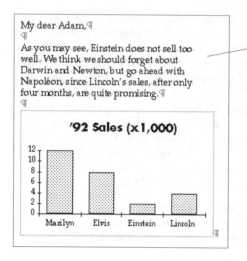

COPY/PASTE OBJECT

Copy the table or chart inside Excel. Shift-scroll Word 5's **Edit** menu and choose the **Paste Object** command.

For this example, a small table was created inside an Excel worksheet, then selected to make a chart.

The object appears at the Insertion Point. It reacts like a picture. When Show ¶ is on, it is surrounded by a dotted border.

EDIT OBJECT

Double-clicking the object displays it inside an Excel window, where you can use all the Excel features and menu commands to edit the object.

Closing this window activates the Word 5 document, which now includes the changed object.

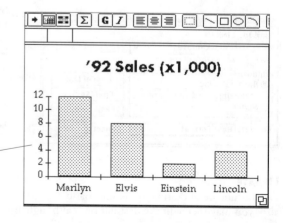

When you choose the **Object...** command of the **Insert** menu and select *Excel Worksheet* in the dialog box below, Word 5 opens an object window belonging to Excel.

As soon as you close this window, the table you've created appears in the Word 5 document as an *Embedded Object*.

If you want a chart rather than a table, it is easier to create it within Excel as explained on the opposite page and paste it than to choose the *Excel Chart* option in the dialog box below. This opens an empty Excel chart window, and you need to use Excel's **Series...** menu command to create the chart's bars

OBJECT TYPE

This list shows all the applications present on your hard disk that support OLE (*Object Linking and Embedding*), i.e. can be opened by Word 5.

Such an application declares itself as OLE-friendly in the *Preferences* folder of the System folder the first time it is run.

So if a brand new never-run Excel is located on your hard disk, it won't be listed until you run it once.

Word appears here because it supports OLE, but it is not very interesting to *Paste Object* from Word to Word. From Word to Excel is possible, of course.

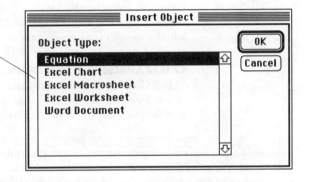

OPTIONS

Select the object and choose the **Object Options...** command of the **Edit** menu to see this dialog box.

An Excel chart as an embedded object may look like a picture, but it contains as much Excel info as a separate Excel document. This can increase the size of your Word 5 document considerably. When you know you won't edit the object anymore, you may discard the Excel info and reduce the size of your document by clicking the *Freeze Picture* button. The object then becomes a simple picture.

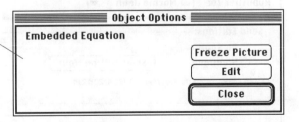

79

EXAMPLES

This is a way to link a source called a *Publisher* to a destination called a *Subscriber*. The source and the destination can belong to different applications supporting the *Publish/Subscribe* feature (like Word 5, QuarkXPress 3.1, Illustrator 3.2, etc.) and to different Macintosh computers on the same network.

As you can't expect all applications to communicate together, the linking is done through a special kind of System 7 document called an *Edition*. Word 5 doesn't know QuarkXPress 3.1, but it knows how to *Publish an Edition* and how to *Subscribe* to one.

EDITION

Editions have wide rectangular icons.

Some text is selected, then the **Create Publisher...** command of the **Edit** menu is chosen. A dialog box including a *Preview* of the Edition, similar to the one on the opposite page but with a *Publish* button, lets you name the Edition and save it where you want (i.e., possibly on some other Macintosh with a *Shared Folder*, etc.)

QUARKXPRESS 3.1 SUBSCRIBER

QuarkXPress 3.1 can only subscribe to pictures. It did accept to subscribe to the *NormaJean* Edition: the text below is in fact a QuarkXPress picture box. When you edit the publisher (in Word 5), this "picture" is changed instantly

Lesta and I have started going to school. It is only four blocks away from Ida's house. We walk the four blocks with Susan Preger. She is a big girl, already in third grade. And Tippy always comes with us. He waits for me at the door of the school and I am sure to find him when I come out. He is so glad to see me, he yelps and jumps and licks my face with his gooey tongue. Oh, I love it!

PUBLISHER OPTIONS

Select the Publisher text (which is surrounded by brackets like a source link) and choose the **Publisher Options...** command of the **Edit** menu to see this dialog box. Default updating of Edition is whenever you save.

Links: Publish/Subscribe

Several people can subscribe to the same Edition. As the NormaJean Edition was saved in a Shared Folder, it was subscribed to not only by the QuarkXPress document used to make this book, but also by a Word 5 document located on another Macintosh. You may notice below that the selected NormaJean line is not black, but grey: the other Macintosh has a colour screen, and this line is in fact blue.

BABY
The Edition named *Baby* contains an Illustrator 3.2 picture. When the line is selected, a scaled version of the picture appears under *Preview*.

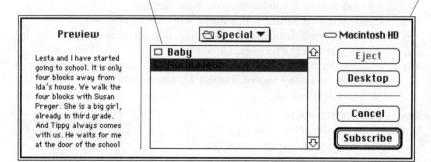

SUBSCRIBE
Choosing the **Subscribe To…** command in the **Edit** menu of Word 5 opens this dialog box, which lets you look for Editions in your hard disk or on the network. Editions may have been made by other people and bear strange names; thus, the *Preview* feature is very useful.
A Subscriber is surrounded by brackets like a link destination.

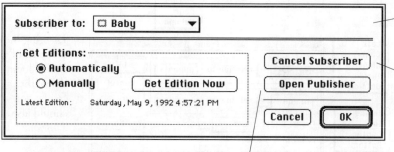

SUBSCRIBER OPTIONS
Default update is automatic.

CANCEL SUBSCRIBER
When you cancel, the Subscriber ceases to be one (it becomes ordinary text or graphics).
You can't throw away an Edition unless you have cancelled all its subscribers.

OPEN PUBLISHER
Opening the Publisher to edit the source is not always possible. For example, in a network situation, an Edition located on some other Macintosh should belong to a shared folder, so that you can access it, but the Publisher behind the Edition may be out of the shared folder; i.e., out of reach.

81

EXAMPLES

The *Frame* feature of Word 5 lets you position elements on the page in a way that is vaguely similar to what DTP (DeskTop Publishing) programs like PageMaker or QuarkXPress can do.

There are two **Frame...** commands. With the **Insert** menu one, you drag a selected element wherever you want in *Print Preview* mode. With the **Format** menu one, you define the position of the element much more precisely in the dialog box below.

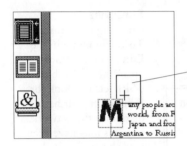

DRAG IN PRINT PREVIEW

Select a letter like this big M (or more text, or a picture), then choose the **Frame...** command of the **Insert** menu.

The display switches to an enlarged *Print Preview*. The letter is surrounded by a dotted border. Inside this border, the Pointer becomes cross-shaped, and you can drag the frame around.

If you stay in the margin, this works very nicely, but if you move the frame to some inhabited zone, the program takes quite a while before it shows you how the text wraps around it.

An element positioned in this manner stays where it is. This wouldn't really do for a *Drop Cap* such as this M, which you expect to move up or down with edited text.

PARAGRAPH PROPERTIES MARK

You can recognize a frame in Normal or Page Layout view by its square *Paragraph Properties Mark*. Double-click the mark to open the dialog box below.

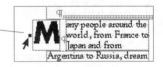

FRAME DIALOG BOX

Whereas dragging a frame in *Print Preview* defines an *absolute* position, the **Frame...** command of the **Format** menu offers *absolute* positions (when you choose Page in the pop-up menus) or *relative* ones.

A Drop Cap should be *In Line*, for example, the better to follow the movements of the main text.

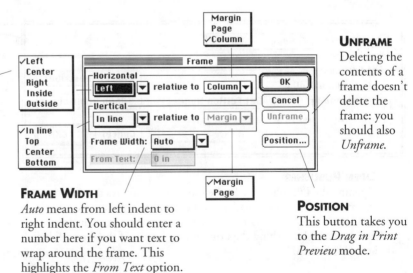

FRAME WIDTH

Auto means from left indent to right indent. You should enter a number here if you want text to wrap around the frame. This highlights the *From Text* option.

UNFRAME

Deleting the contents of a frame doesn't delete the frame: you should also *Unframe*.

POSITION

This button takes you to the *Drag in Print Preview* mode.

Dragging a frame… Adjusting its position in the Frame dialog box… Dragging again… Adjusting again… You may get nice enough results, like below, but you lose a lot of time wondering why things don't look the way you expected.

By and by, you learn to go along with what Word 5 is willing to do rather than try to impose your design.

HEADER
An empty one-line paragraph with grey shading.

DROP CAP
Horizontal: 0.94 "
Relative to the Page.
Vertical:
In Line.
0.5" Width.
0.1" from Text.

BODY COPY
A separate three-column division.

FOOTER
Controlling the height of a Header or Footer is possible but lengthy.
The two lines at the bottom do not belong to the Footer, but to a separate one-column division.

TITLE
Small Caps, one-column division.

BLACKMOUSE
A picture frame here would push back the title. Instead, the picture is a character, subscripted by 35 pt.

COUPON
Five paragraphs selected together, bordered and framed together. The frame was dragged to its position in *Print Preview* mode. This kind of multi-paragraph frame is subject to an illness which the Word 5 manual calls *Items Overlapping,* especially when you try to change the initial positioning.
This is cured by going back to Normal View and positioning again. In severe cases, unframe before re-positioning.

"ENGLISH IS EASY", SAYS BLACK MOUSE.

Many people around the world, from France to Japan and from Argentina to Russia, dream of learning English. Their dream can't turn into reality because they lack time, willpower, or enough money to go into "full-immersion" courses or spend a year in the States. Some are entitled to free lessons inside their company, some study schoolbook-type manuals by themselves. This is very boring, and reminds them of the time they wasted in school.

Indeed, most people have studied English in school for several years. Some have visited England or America. They probably know enough to survive in London or New York City, or would remember enough after a few days there, but what they really need is something else: they need to understand written English.

In many fields, from computers to advertising,

from medicine to the movies, technical information and updating is given in books and magazines published in English and seldom translated into other languages.

People often spend one hour every day in subways or local trains. If you study anything one hour per day (be it piano, karate or Black Mouse books), visible or audible results can't fail to materialize after a while. The key to success is continuity: you shouldn't stop. This implies that the activity is pleasurable.

Since readers begin with a scant knowledge of English and aim for a perfect grasp, we have

made our books "progressive". For example, in her mock autobiography, Marilyn Monroe begins with a baby's thoughts and talk, then grows up to utter slightly longer sentences.

Whereas French or Japanese people don't usually know a word of Farsi or Tamoul, they are familiar with many words of English, because they have not forgotten *everything* they studied in school and because songs and movies keep refreshing their memories. So they could undoubtedly read the first pages of Marilyn's story.

Other mock memoirs are available: Elvis Presley, Einstein, etc.

Please send me more Info about Black Mouse mock biographies.
Name...
Address..
City.................... Country....................
Black Mouse, 22 rue du petit musc 75004 Paris France

Black Mouse mock biographies. A series of easy and entertaining books for people who want to learn English or improve their knowledge of the language.

EXAMPLES

Adding commands to Word menus is great! The only drawback is that when you work with other programs, you feel frustrated because they don't offer this wonderful feature.

A fast and easy way is shown below, a more elaborate method on the opposite page.

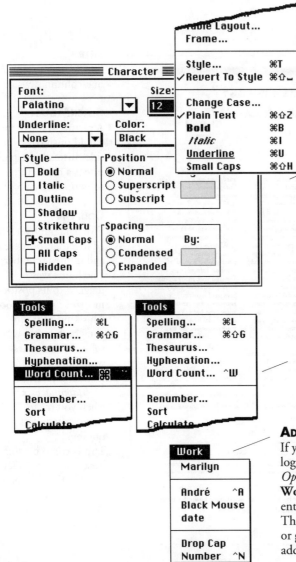

ADD A COMMAND

When you press Option, Command and the *keyboard* +/= sign, the Pointer becomes a big fat **+**.

Click an item on the ribbon or ruler, or a dialog box option, with this **+** to add it as a command to the menu it logically belongs to.

Here, clicking **Small Caps** in the Character dialog box adds it to the **Format** menu with its default shortcut.

If you're not happy with the default menu and shortcut, see the opposite page.

To delete a command, press Option, Command and the keyboard – sign. The pointer becomes a big **–**. Scroll a menu and

ADD A SHORTCUT

When you press Option, Command and the *numeric keypad* + sign, the Pointer becomes a big fat .

Scroll a menu and choose a command with this . An alert box asks you to press the keys you want for the shortcut.

Here, the frequently used **Word Count...** command was chosen, and the Control and W keys were pressed. The shortcut appears as **^W**.

ADD A MENU

If you click a document name inside an *Open* dialog box with the **+** Pointer (and also click the *Open* button), the program adds it inside a new **Work** menu. Same thing for a glossary name or entry, or a style in the **Style** pop-up menu.

This menu makes it very easy to open documents or glossary entries. It becomes even easier if you add shortcuts.

84

By default, the commands and menus you design here are saved in the Setting(5) file and apply to all the documents you open with Word 5. The *Save as...* button at the bottom of the dialog box lets you create other settings files.

When several settings files have been created, you can choose which one will apply by clicking the *Open...* button, or by double-clicking the file you want on the Desktop.

COMMANDS

This list includes several hundred commands. As in all dialog box lists, you reach a letter quickly by typing it. Select a command to see its description, its default menu and shortcuts. If the command is present in a menu, the *Add* button is dimmed and *Remove* is highlighted.

MENU LIST

Screen Test command belongs to **Tools** menu, but you can choose another menu if you want.

ADD BELOW

Auto means *Wherever Word 5 wishes.* Pop-up menu also says **Top** and **Bottom**, and offers a full list of the **Tools** menu commands. Choose one to put **Screen Test** just under it.

DO IT

Selecting a command in the list and clicking *Do It* is similar to choosing a command in a menu.

This is a way to choose some exotic command, which you don't want to add to any menu but do need once in a while.

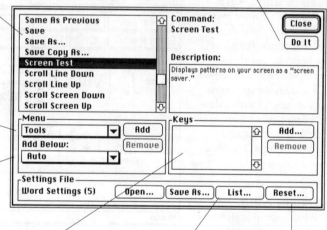

KEYS/ADD

Clicking this button displays the *Press the keys you want* alert box. You might choose a shortcut for **Screen Test** even if you don't add it to a menu: you will then be able to choose the command by using the shortcut.

Before doing this, you could press the key combination you have in mind to check whether it already corresponds to a command. If it does, the command will be selected. You may retain the shortcut for **Screen Test**, but then the former command will lose it.

LIST

This button lets you create a new Word document containing either the list of commands in the menus, or a full list of available Word 5 commands with default menus and shortcuts.

RESET

You can revert to the original Word 5 settings, or to the last *Settings* file.

One option lets you add *all* the commands to their default menus. This was used as a starting point for the menus' pictures on p. 92 and 93.

APPENDIX

The Equation Editor is a separate program (a special version of a program called *Math Type*). You may use it without Word 5, and paste equations as pictures into MacWrite or QuarkXPress.

With Word 5 and System 7, you don't paste equations, because the Equation Editor supports OLE. You open it from the *Insert Object* dialog box (see p. 79) and design your equation. When you close the object window, the equation appears in the Word document at the Insertion point.

You double-click the equation in Word to edit it inside the object window.

PALETTES

First line of ten pop-up menus (called *Palettes* in the Equation Editor manual) offers you *Symbols*, second line offers *Templates* (see opposite page).

A template, e.g. an Integral or Square Root sign, contains rectangles with a dotted border called *Slots*. You enter letters, numbers, symbols or other templates into the slots.

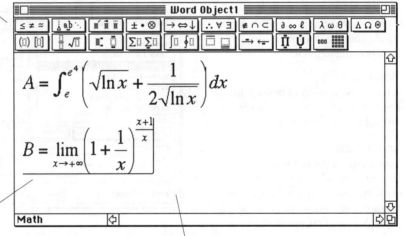

INSERTION POINT

The half rectangle around the B equation is actually the Insertion point.

Its horizontal part always shows the bottom of the active slot; the vertical part shows where the next character will appear.

You move it from one slot to another by clicking or, better, by pressing the Tab key.

A AND B

It only takes a few minutes to write these two equations.

When you type lnx, the program identifies ln as a function (to be written in roman) and x as a variable (in italics). It enlarges the parentheses, which are *Templates*, when you fill the slots, etc.

The default fonts are Times and Symbol. As Times is slightly smaller than Symbol, the manual suggests you replace it with Bookman or New Century Schoolbook if you use a lot of Greek letters. This is done with the **Define...** command of the program's **Style** menu.

By default, the equations are displayed at 200% enlargement. Thus they become twice smaller in Word. You can also choose a 100 or 400% display in the program's **View** menu.

The Equation Editor comes with its own clear manual and Help file. It also has its own elaborate collection of shortcuts.

This program is very easy to use if you let it do the thinking and the choosing. You do need to study the manual if you want to do things your own way. For example, if you work in a field where a certain C_b^a function is used, you must select the C and choose **Text** in the **Style** menu, otherwise the program thinks it is a variable and sets it in italic.

SYMBOL PALETTES

From Left to right: relational symbols; spaces and ellipses (as the space bar can't be used for symbols inside slots, a 1/3 em space was inserted in this way between the right parenthesis and dx in the A equation); overbars/primes/vector arrows; operators; arrows; logical symbols; set theory symbols; miscellaneous symbols; Greek lowercase and uppercase.

TEMPLATE PALETTES

Parentheses/brackets/braces; fractions and radicals; subscript/superscript; integrals; summation; overbar/underbar; labelled arrows; products/set theory symbols; matrices.
When you choose a template in the last line of the matrix palette, a dialog box lets you set the number of rows and columns, and also add borders around and inside the matrix.

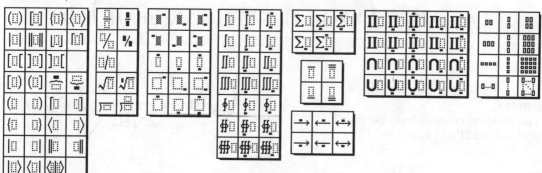

APPENDIX

Formulas were used to write equations in Word 4, i.e. before the Equation Editor made it so easy.

Writing the Integral below took much longer than with the Equation Editor. On the other hand, once the formula is ready, it is possible to edit its elements with full Word character formatting power.

There are only ten basic formula codes, plus a series of *Optional Characters* to modify them, all listed in an appendix of the Word 5 manual. Unless you really want to become a formula buff, you'd better import ready-to-wear formulas with "placeholder" words from the special formula glossary.

FORMULA GLOSSARY

To see this glossary, choose the **Glossary...** command in the **Edit** menu. When the standard glossary is displayed, choose the **Open...** command in the **File** menu and open the Formula glossary in the *Glossaries* folder.

Notice "placeholders" Bottom, Top and Right.

NESTED FORMULAS

To get the special formula character (which you need to type only if you don't use the glossary), press the Option, Command and \ keys.

Notice nested formulas and parentheses: \R for Square Root inside \F for Fraction inside \I for Integral.

PARAGRAPH MARKS

You must be in Normal view and display the ¶ marks to create the formula.

$$A = \backslash I(_{e},e^{4},\Big(\backslash R(\ln x) + \backslash F(1,2\backslash R(\ln x)) \Big) \, dx)$$

INTEGRAL

This is what the formula looks like with ¶ marks off or in Page Layout view.

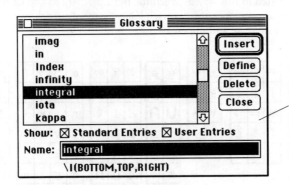

$$A = \int_{e}^{e^{4}} \left(\sqrt{\ln x} + \frac{1}{2\sqrt{\ln x}} \right) dx$$

88

Formulas, PostScript

The *PostScript* glossary contains entries like *Crop Marks, Line Between Columns, Margin Note*, etc. *Word Under Text* was tested for the example below.

When you choose an entry in the glossary, PostScript code appears at the Insertion point in your Word document, in *Hidden Text* style. You may write such code yourself if you know how to, or change easy-to-recognize items.

It seems that Lesta's name should be written Lester, and mine Norma Jean. When I was baptized by Della they wrote it Norma Jeane, but maybe it was a mistake.

```
% Word Under Text
/Times-BoldItalic findfont
/FontSize 72 def
/TextToPrint (CONFIDENTIAL) def
FontSize scalefont setfont
/printDraft
{0 0 moveto TextToPrint show} def
wp$x 2 div wp$y 2 div translate
45 rotate
TextToPrint stringwidth pop 2 div neg
FontSize 2 mul 3 div 2 div neg
translate
.95 -.05 .6
{setgray printDraft -1 .5 translate} for
.9 setgray printDraft
```

Every morning we pray God before the class begins. In the prayer God is called "Our father in Heaven". I don't know where this Heaven is, but all the other children seem to also have a father in Los Angeles.

WORD UNDER TEXT

Choosing the *Word Under Text* entry inserts this hidden text. You may set the Insertion point anywhere on the page, as a default PostScript effect applies to the page.

This default code prints the word *Confidential* in Times BoldItalic at 45° across the page.

---

waits for me at the door of the school and I am sure to find him when I come out. He is so glad to see me, he yelps and jumps and licks my face with his gooey tongue. Oh, how I love it!

We learn to read and write. It is quite difficult. At first, we only learn words with three letters, like dog, cat, bed, red, hot, nut, bad, hat, fat, god, log, man, sad, tip, lip, lap, pet, bat, hip, wet, mud, rug. You just write them the way you hear them.

It seems that Lesta's name should be written Lester, and mine Norma Jean. When I was baptized by Della they wrote it Norma Jeane, but maybe it was a mistake.

Every morning we pray God before the class begins. In the prayer God is called "Our father in Heaven." I don't know where this Heaven is, but all the other children seem to also have a father in Los Angeles. "Mama, where is my father?" I asked Gladys. She answered that he was very far away.

These other children simply live in houses with their mothers and fathers. Why do I live with people who are not even my real aunt and uncle?

Maybe Gladys is not really my mother. I am the daughter of a beautiful Prince and a sweet Princess, who are going to come some day and take me away to their marble palace. So then I shall pull my tongue at all these kids who live in tiny houses with their stupid parents.

TRUE STORY

This is what the document looks like when printed: you can't see the PostScript effect before printing, and of course you don't see anything if the printer doesn't support PostScript.

The word *Confidential* was replaced by *True Story*, Times-BoldItalic was replaced by Helvetica-Bold and 45° by 30°.

INDEX

Index

MENUS

All commands with shortcuts, as well as some other useful ones, have been added to the menus here. You can use the shortcuts even when the commands are not added to the menus.

See default menus on p. 38, 44, 46, 48, 54, 58, 60 and 66.

File

New	⌘N
Open...	⌘O
Open Any File...	⇧F6
Close	⌘W
Save	⌘S
Save As...	⇧F7
Save Copy As...	
Delete...	
Find File...	
Summary Info...	
Print Preview...	⌘⌥I
Page Setup...	⇧F8
Print...	⌘P
✓Fractional Widths	
Print Merge...	
Open Mail...	
Send Mail...	
Quit	⌘Q

MAIL
You need
Microsoft Mail
to use these
commands.

Edit

Undo Copy	⌘Z
Repeat Typing	⌘Y
Cut	⌘X
Copy	⌘C
Copy as Picture	⌘⌥D
Paste	⌘V
Paste Link	⌥F4
Paste Cells	
Paste Special...	
Paste Object	⌘F4
Clear	
Select All	⌘A
Delete Forward	⌘⌥F
Delete Next Word	⌘⌥G
Delete Previous Word	⌘⌥⌫
Copy Text	⌘⌥C
Move Text	⌘⌥X
Copy Formats	⌘⌥V
Paste Special Character	⌘⌥Q
Change Font	⌘⇧E
✓Change Style	⌘⇧S
Find...	⌘F
Find Again	⌘⌥A
Find Formats	
Replace...	⌘H
Go To...	⌘G
Go Back	⌘⌥Z
Glossary...	⌘K
Insert Glossary Entry	⌘⌫
Create Publisher...	
Subscribe To...	
Link Options...	
Update Link	⌥F3
Edit Object...	
Demote Heading	
Promote Heading	
Move Heading Down	
Move Heading Up	
Make Body Text	
Outline Command Prefix	⌘⌥T
Activate Keyboard Menus	⌘➜|

View

✓Normal	⌘⌥N
Outline	⌘⌥O
Page Layout	⌘⌥P
✓Ribbon	⌘⌥R
✓Ruler	⌘R
Print Merge Helper...	
Quick Record Voice Annotation	
Show ¶	⌘J
Header	
Footer	
Split Window	⌘⌥S
Footnotes	⌘⇧⌥S
Voice Annotations	
Footnote Separator...	
Footnote Cont. Separator...	
Footnote Cont. Notice...	
✓Show Hidden Text	
Show Picture Placeholders	
✓Show Table Gridlines	
Show Text Boundaries	
Open Documents in Page View	
Expand Subtext	
Collapse Subtext	
Show Heading 1	
Show Heading 2	
Show Heading 3	
Show Heading 4	
Show All Headings	
Collapse Selection	
✓Show Formatting	
Show Body Text	

Insert

Page Break	⇧⌥~
Section Break	⌘⌥~
Line Break	⇧↵
New Paragraph	↵
New ¶ After Ins. Point	⌘⌥↵
Table...	
Table to Text...	
Text to Table...	
Footnote...	⌘E
New ¶ with Same Style	⌘↵
Voice Annotation	
Date	
Page Number	
Time	
Symbol...	
Insert ¶ Above Row	⌘⌥_
Insert Nonbreaking Hyphen	⌘`
Insert Optional Hyphen	⌘-
Insert Nonbreaking Space	⌥_
Insert Formula	⌘⌥\
Insert Tab	➜|
Index Entry	
Index...	
TOC Entry	
Table of Contents...	
Frame...	
File...	
Picture...	
New Picture	
Object...	

92

Format

Character...	⌘D
Paragraph...	⌘M
Tabs...	
Section...	⍀F14
Document...	⌘F14
Border...	
Table Cells...	
Table Layout...	
Insert Columns	
Delete Columns	
Insert Rows	^⌘V
Delete Rows	^⌘X
Frame...	
Style...	⌘T
Redefine Style From Selection	
✓Revert To Style	⌘⇧_
Change Case...	
Uppercase	
Lowercase	
Title Case	
Sentence Case	
Toggle Case	
✓Plain Text	⌘⇧Z
Bold	⌘B
Italic	⌘I
Underline	⌘U
Word Underline	⌘⇧]
Double Underline	⌘⇧[
Dotted Underline	⌘⇧\
Strikethru	⌘⇧/
Outline	⌘⇧D
Shadow	⌘⇧W
Small Caps	⌘⇧H
All Caps	⌘⇧K
Hidden Text	⌘⇧V
Superscript 3 pt	⌘⇧=
Subscript 2 pt	⌘⇧-
Condensed 1.5 pt	
Expanded 3 pt	
✓Black	
Blue	
Cyan	
Green	
Magenta	
Red	
Yellow	
White	
✓Normal Paragraph	⌘⇧P
✓Paragraph Aligned Left	⌘⇧L
Centered	⌘⇧C
Paragraph Aligned Right	⌘⇧R
Justified	⌘⇧J
✓Line Spacing: Single	
Line Spacing: 1 and 1/2	
Line Spacing: Double	⌘⇧Y
Space Before ¶: 12 points	⌘⇧0
First Line Indent	⌘⇧F
Hanging Indent	⌘⇧T
Nest Paragraph	⌘⇧N
Unnest Paragraph	⌘⇧M
Suppress Line # in Paragraph	
L Thick Paragraph Border	⌘⍀2
No Paragraph Border	⌘⍀1

Font

9 Point	
10 Point	
✓12 Point	
14 Point	
18 Point	
24 Point	
Smaller Font Size	⌘⇧<
Larger Font Size	⌘⇧>
Up	⌘]
Down	⌘[
Other...	
Default Font...	
AGaramond	
AGaramond Bold	
AGaramond BoldItalic	
AGaramond Italic	

Window

Help...	
Show Clipboard	
Zoom Window	⌘⍀]
Move to Next Window	⌘⍀W
New Window	⇧F5
Zoom to Fill Screen	
✓Untitled1	

Tools

Spelling...	⌘L
Grammar...	⌘⇧G
Thesaurus...	
Hyphenation...	⇧F15
Word Count...	⍀F15
Renumber...	⌘F15
Sort	
Sort Descending	
Calculate	⌘=
Repaginate Now	
Screen Test	
Numeric Lock	⌨⌫
Preferences...	
Commands...	⌘⇧⍀C
Add to Menu	⌘⍀=
Remove From Menu	⌘⍀-
Assign to Key	⌘⍀⌨+
Unassign Keystroke	⌘⍀⌨-
Move to Start of Document	⌘⌨9
Move to End of Document	⌘⌨3
Move to Previous Character	←
Move to Next Character	→
Move to Previous Word	⌘←
Move to Next Word	⌘→
Move to Previous Sentence	⌘⌨7
Move to Next Sentence	⌘⌨1
Move to Previous Paragraph	⌘↑
Move to Next Paragraph	⌘↓
Move to Previous Line	↑
Move to Next Line	↓
Move to Start of Line	⌨7
Move to End of Line	⌨1
Scroll Screen Up	⌨9
Scroll Screen Down	⍀.
Move to Top of Window	⌘⌨5
Move to Bottom of Window	end
Scroll Line Up	⌘⍀[
Scroll Line Down	⌘⍀/
Extend to Character	⌘⍀H
Move to Next Cell	
Move to Previous Cell	⇧→⊦

93

SPECIAL

We thought you might be interested in examining and studying the various Marilyn mockfiles used as examples in this book. A floppy disk containing these files will be sent to you as soon as we receive your name and address and a payment by cheque for £6.95, which will include VAT & postage.

Thank you

Write to: Marilyn Disk,

Computer Generation Ltd,

3, Adam & Eve Mews, London W8 6UG

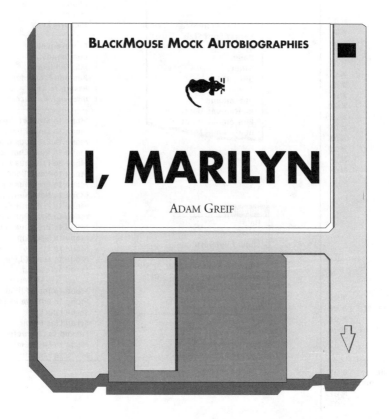

BLACKMOUSE MOCK AUTOBIOGRAPHIES

I, MARILYN

ADAM GREIF

Marilyn Disk

All the files except the Marilyn story have been created for this book. Some only contain two or three paragraphs, which is usually enough to explain one function or more.

Futura Bold font has been used here and there. When a title is not displayed in a satisfactory manner, select it and try Helvetica or Times.

MARILYN
Thirty-six pages tell the true story of Marilyn Monroe's childhood and youth. If you order the Marilyn Disk, we'll have your name and address, so we'll keep you informed about the story's eventual completion and publication!

TABLES
Table can be seen on p. 35.

MARILYNLETTER
Letter to publishers, merged with *USPublishers* address list. See p. 74.

OUTLINING
Very short example for p. 72.

USPUBLISHERS
Three addresses in a table, to be merged with *MarilynLetter*.

CATALOG
A document with links within itself and with *#BlackMouse*. See p. 76.

NORMAJEAN
An *Edition* for Publish/Subscribe example on p. 80.

#BLACKMOUSE
One line only in this document, created for the *Link* example.

EMBEDDED CHART
Object example on p. 78.

BLACKMOUSEAD
DTP example on p. 83.

CALCULUS
Two versions of the same equation: one was created with the Equation Editor, and can be double-clicked (see p. 86); the other one is made with Formulas (see p. 88).

MARILYNSETTINGS
Double-clicking this icon opens an Untitled document with the gigantic menus displayed on p. 92 and 93 (see also p. 85).

Marilyn

Tables

MarilynLetter

Outlining

Catalog

USPublishers

NormaJean

#BlackMouse

BlackMouseAd

Embedded chart

Calculus

MarilynSettings

95

CONTENTS

Semi-resident 0-4-2 FINN MacCOOL, built by TMA Engineering in 1986, starts its train away from Much Natter station on the Beer Heights Light Railway. 26th August 2015.

Some Useful References:

- "Miniature Railways of Great Britain and Ireland" by Peter Bryant and Dave Holroyde, published in 2012 by Platform 5 Publishing. ISBN 978 190233 693 0.
- "Tiny Trains, A Guide to Britain's Miniature Railways", published annually by Marksman Publications.
- Various editions of Ian Allan's "Miniature Railways" by Robin Butterell et al.
- The "Miniature Railway World" website: www.miniaturerailwayworld.co.uk

INTRODUCTION

In this, the second volume of "Miniature Railway Album", we look at railways with gauges below one foot, from $10\frac{1}{4}$ inches down to the 5 and $3\frac{1}{2}$ inch gauge tracks that are popular with model engineering societies.

There are many fine railways that operate on these gauges, including the $10\frac{1}{4}$ inch gauge Audley End Miniature Railway, the Eastleigh Lakeside Steam Railway, the Stapleford Miniature Railway and the Wells and Walsingham Light Railway. Among the most notable of the $7\frac{1}{4}$ inch gauge lines are the Beer Heights Light Railway, the Great Cockcrow Railway and the Moors Valley Railway. We look at all of these railways and many others, but the Eastleigh Lakeside Steam Railway and the Moors Valley Railway receive more extensive coverage because of the photographic opportunities and the variety of motive power available on these two lines.

$10\frac{1}{4}$ inch gauge railways became popular early on and, as a consequence, many historic locomotives are still operating today, having moved from railway to railway over the years. The Eastleigh Lakeside Steam Railway, in particular, has a fine collection. Locomotives on the $7\frac{1}{4}$ inch gauge railways are often of more recent construction, although there are, of course, many exceptions. The $7\frac{1}{4}$ inch gauge Moors Valley Railway has an impressive fleet of large narrow gauge style locomotives which the driver can sit in, rather than on. The earliest of these dates back to 1968, but most are more recent.

The locomotives and trains that can be found on these railways are both interesting and varied, depending on whether they are based on standard or narrow gauge prototypes, or do not owe their design to any full size prototype at all. The majority of these railways are transitory, as is easy to see if one looks at some of the old Ian Allan ABCs, and I, for one, regret not having spent more time visiting these railways in years gone by. I also wonder what the future will hold as people's interests and hobbies change in this increasingly electronics based world.

I have spent many enjoyable days visiting the small railways of England and Wales and producing these books. It is my hope that some of that pleasure is shared with those reading them.

Peter J. Green
Worcester, England
2019

AUDLEY END
MINIATURE RAILWAY

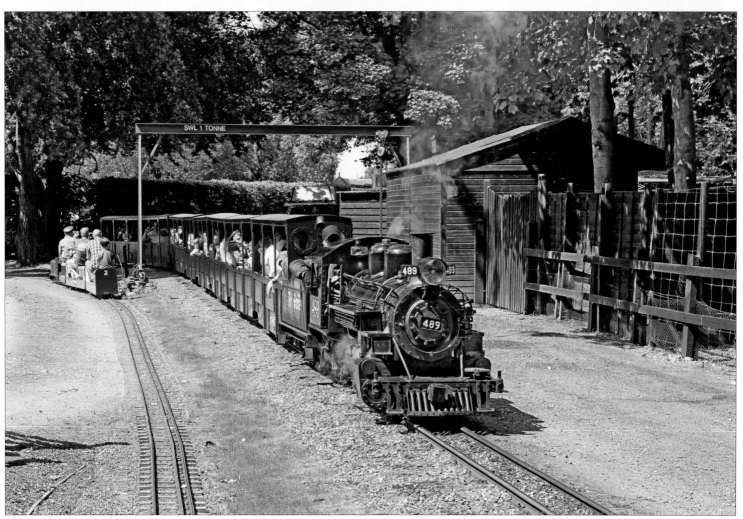

Opened in 1964, Lord Braybrooke's 10¹/₄ inch gauge Audley End Miniature Railway runs for 1mile at Audley End House, Saffron Walden in Essex. Here 2-8-2 No. 489 SARA LUCY heads its train away from Audley End station. The line is a dumb-bell with Audley End station located on the balloon loop next to the car park. SARA LUCY is based on a Denver and Rio Grande K36 class locomotive and was built in 1977 by David Curwen. The train on the left is running on the track of the Saffron Walden and District Society of Model Engineers. 7th June 2015.

0-4-0+0-4-0 diesel-hydraulic No. 691 HENRIETTA JANE heads a train into the balloon loop on the approach to Audley End station. HENRIETTA JANE was built by A. Crowhurst in 1991. 7th June 2015.

David Curwen 2-6-2 No. 24 BRUCE of 1991 approaches Audley End station during the 2016 Steam Gala. 18th September 2016.

Visiting from the Wimbish Light Railway, 4-6-0 No. 6100 ROYAL SCOT heads a train away from Audley End station during the 2016 Steam Gala. No. 6100 was built by Winkler Engineering of Southampton in 1963. 18th September 2016.

The dual gauge 5 inch and $7^1/_4$ inch track of the Saffron Walden and District Society of Model Engineers is located next to the $10^1/_4$ inch gauge track of the Audley End Miniature Railway. Visiting $7^1/_4$ inch gauge single Fairlie 0-4-4T, Swanley New Barn Railway No. 11 ANEIRIN, built by P. Beevers in 2014, heads an empty train along the line. 18th September 2016.

BICKINGTON STEAM RAILWAY

Opened in 1988, the Bickington Steam Railway runs for 1³/₄ miles through Trago Central from Riverside station, next to the car park. There is a balloon loop at the top end of the line as well as a small halt. A complete passenger journey over the railway is 2¹/₄ miles. The railway is located at the Trago Mills Shopping and Leisure Centre, near Newton Abbot. Here, 2-6-0 ALICE approaches Riverside station with the stock for the first train of the day. ALICE was built in 1984 by Simkins and Vere. 27th May 2015.

BRESSINGHAM

Opened in 1995, the $10\frac{1}{4}$ inch gauge Garden Railway runs for 700 yards, with a balloon loop, through the gardens at Bressingham Steam Museum in Norfolk. There is also a 15 inch gauge line at the museum. 0-4-0ST No. 1 ALAN BLOOM approaches the station with a Garden Railway train. VR 2-8-0 No. 1144 from Finland is in the background. ALAN BLOOM was built in 1995 by P. Gray. 27th May 2016.

Nearly eight years before the photograph on the previous page, ALAN BLOOM is pictured at work in red livery. 25th August 2008.

A 9$\frac{1}{2}$ inch gauge line, opened in 1964, ran round the gardens before the present day 10$\frac{1}{4}$ inch gauge line was built. Here 4-6-2 No. 1 PRINCESS, built by the Motor Gear and Engineering Co. in 1947, is seen at work. No. 1 formerly operated at Danson Park, Bexley Heath. August 1969.

CATTLE COUNTRY RAILWAY

Opened in 2005, the 10$\frac{1}{4}$ inch gauge Cattle Country Railway makes a circuit of about a mile within the Cattle Country Adventure Park at Berkeley in Gloucestershire. There is also a spur to Oakhill Station. The steam outline 0-6-2 diesel-hydraulic is pictured soon after leaving the main station and crossing the mini Severn Bridge. The locomotive was built by Joe Nemeth in 2008. 23rd May 2015.

EASTLEIGH LAKESIDE RAILWAY

Opened in 1992, the 10¼ and 7¼ inch dual gauge Eastleigh Lakeside Steam Railway makes a 1¼ mile circuit within the Lakeside Country Park at Eastleigh In Hampshire. There are two stations, Eastleigh Parkway, next to the car park, and Monks Brook Halt. The railway is home to a fine collection of locomotives of both gauges.

7¼ inch gauge 2-6-2 No. 10 SIR ARTHUR HEYWOOD, heads a birthday special on the Eastleigh Lakeside Railway. This locomotive was built by K. Williamson in 1984. It is a half scale model of NORTHERN ROCK on the Ravenglass and Eskdale Railway. 22nd March 2009.

Herbert Bullock built the four large 10¼ inch gauge Great Western style 4-6-2s that currently operate on the Eastleigh Lakeside Railway. Here, three of the locomotives head a train towards Eastleigh Parkway. They are No. 2006 EDWARD VIII of 1936, No. 1002 THE EMPRESS of 1933, and No. 1001 THE MONARCH of 1932. 22nd March 2009.

10¼ inch gauge locomotives 4-6-0 No. 850 LORD NELSON and 4-4-2 No.1908 ERNEST HENRY UPTON approach Eastleigh Parkway station. LORD NELSON was built in 2007 by Jesse Moody. ERNEST HENRY UPTON was built by G & S Light Engineering in 1937. This locomotive previously worked at Dudley Zoo and Weymouth. 22nd March 2009.

7¼ inch gauge locomotives 4-4-2 No. 4789 WILLIAM BAKER and No. 4 FRANCIS HENRY LLOYD double-head a train back to Eastleigh Parkway. WILLIAM BAKER was built in 1947 and is named after its builder. FRANCIS HENRY LLOYD was built in 1959 by G & S Light Engineering and F. H. Lloyd and Co. for the Hilton Valley Railway, moving to the Weston Park Railway after the Hilton Valley Railway was closed. 23rd March 2014.

10¼ inch gauge 2-4-2 No. 7 SANDY RIVER exits the tunnel as it heads for Eastleigh Parkway. SANDY RIVER was built in 1983 by A. Bimpson. 22nd March 2009.

10¼ inch gauge 4-6-0 No. 6100 ROYAL SCOT is turned at Eastleigh Parkway. No. 6100 was built by Carland Engineering in 1950. It previously worked at Syon Park. 23rd March 2014.

10¼ inch gauge Bullock 4-6-2 No. 2005 SILVER JUBILEE heads a train round the curve at the end of the long straight from Monks Brook Halt. Built in 1935 by H. Bullock, this locomotive was one of seven built between 1931 and 1937. It previously ran on various railways including the Surrey Border and Camberley Railway and the Kerr's Miniature Railway. SILVER JUBILEE is on long term loan to the Eastleigh Lakeside Railway. 8th June 2013.

10¼ inch gauge 4-6-2 No. 4498 SIR NIGEL GRESLEY at work. This loco was built by William Kirkland in 1967, and previously ran at Thoresby Hall and Stapleford Park. 13th October 2012.

10¼ inch gauge 4-6-2 No. 6220 CORONATION, built by E. Dove in 1946, heads its train away from the tunnel. This locomotive previously ran at Syon Park, Brentford. 3rd May 2009.

With a rainbow in the sky, 10¼ inch gauge 4-6-2 No. 1002 THE EMPRESS rounds the curve away from the double track section, as it heads its train back to Eastleigh Parkway station. 13th October 2012.

10¼ inch gauge locomotives 4-6-2 No. 21C1 CHANNEL PACKET, built by Jesse Moody in 2011, and B-B diesel-hydraulic D1994 EASTLEIGH, built at the ELSR in 1994, stand at Eastleigh Parkway station. SIR NIGEL GRESLEY is in the background. 29th September 2012.

7¼ inch gauge 2-6-2T No. 761 TAW, built by J. Horsfield in 1999, heads its train towards Eastleigh Parkway. 13th October 2012.

No. 8 DAVID CURWEN and Romulus 0-4-0 SANJO top and tail their train near the tunnel. DAVID CURWEN was built by David Curwen in 1972 and previously worked on the Dobwalls Railway. SANJO was built by S. Battle in 1993. Both locomotives are 7¼ inch gauge. 23rd March 2014.

INGFIELD LIGHT RAILWAY

Opened in 1973, the 10¼ inch gauge Ingfield Light Railway is located at Ingfield Manor School, near Billingshurst in West Sussex. The railway is private but is occasionally open to the public, notably during the annual fete in June. The railway runs from Haven Road station through Garden Crossing Halt to Ingfield Central. From here, the railway continues through Marsh Halt, Bramble Hill and Highbeech to the terminus at Hazel End. Schools class 4-4-0 No. 905 TONBRIDGE, built circa 2005, approaches Haven Road with a train from Bramble Hill. 14th June 2015.

10¼ inch gauge Midland Compound 4-4-0 No.1102 stands on the turntable at Bramble Hill. The history of No.1102 is not clear, but it was built as a 9¼ inch gauge locomotive in the 1920s and spent most of its first twenty years in India. A Hymek diesel-hydraulic locomotive stands next to the loco shed. 14th June 2015.

An 0-4-0 diesel shunting locomotive stands at Bramble Hill. The lettering on the side reads "Dennis Bates & Co., Engineers & Chandlers, Leamington, Hastings." 14th June 2015.

Two 0-4-0 Lister diesels, No. 2 (*left*) and THUMPER, stand outside the engine shed at Haven Road. 14th June 2015.

0-6-0T Terriers BRIGHTON and No. 84 CROWBOROUGH, both built by Reg Day, stand outside one of the sheds at Bramble Hill station. 14th June 2015.

4-4-2 No. 3292 JOHN TERENCE heads its train away from Bramble Hill towards Marsh Halt. This locomotive was built in 1908 by Mr. J. A Holder's engineer, Grimshaw. It initially worked on the Broome Railway in Worcestershire. 14th June 2015.

JUNGLE EXPRESS

Opened in 1937, the 10¼ inch gauge Jungle Express is a 500 yard circuit around the lake, within the grounds of Paignton Zoo in Devon. Here, the Class 37 outline 4-4w diesel-mechanical locomotive, built by Nicholson and Wedgewood in 1995, heads a train away from Lakeside station. 27th May 2015.

LAPPA VALLEY RAILWAY

The Lappa Valley Railway at St Newlyn East, near Newquay in Cornwall, has miniature railways of three different gauges. The 15 inch gauge line runs on an old standard gauge trackbed from Benny Halt to East Wheal Rose. The 10¼ inch gauge line, opened in 1995, runs from East Wheal Rose for a further 700 yards along the old trackbed, to Newlyn Downs Halt. The 7¼ inch gauge Woodland Railway, opened in 1978, is a 350 yard circuit at East Wheal Rose.

On the 7¼ inch gauge, Mardyke "APT" 4w-4w petrol-hydraulic locomotive, built circa 1982, speeds round the 350 yard oval track at East Wheal Rose. 17th August 2015.

10¼ inch gauge 0-6-0 diesel hydraulic locomotive ERIC waits to depart from Newlyn Downs Halt with a train to East Wheal Rose. ERIC was built by Alan Keef in 2008. 17th August 2015.

10¼ inch gauge 4w-4 petrol hydraulic locomotive DUKE OF CORNWALL, built by Severn Lamb in 1981, stands under a shelter at East Wheal Rose. 17th August 2015.

MORTOCOMBE MINIATURE RAILWAY

Opened in 2005, the dual 10¼ inch and 7¼ inch gauge Mortocombe Miniature Railway runs for 300 yards in County Gardens Garden Centre, at Chilton in Oxfordshire. In this view, 10¼ inch gauge 2-4-2T PHALAENOPSIS, built by the Exmoor Steam Railway in 2008, stands in the station at the Mortocombe Miniature Railway. A 7¼ inch gauge Lister diesel locomotive is in front of the shed. 23rd April 2016.

POOLE PARK RAILWAY

Opened in 1949, the 10¼ inch gauge Poole Park Railway, at Poole in Dorset, runs for 650 yards around the lake, with a spur to the locomotive and carriage shed. 0-4-2 steam outline diesel ELIZABETH heads a train round the lake on the Poole Park Railway. ELIZABETH was built by the Exmoor Steam Railway in 2012. 4th August 2015.

QUEEN'S PARK MINIATURE RAILWAY

Opened in 1976, the 10¼ inch gauge Queen's Park Miniature Railway is a 550 yard circuit around the lake at Queen's Park in Chesterfield. Steam outline diesel hydraulic 2-6-0 PUFFIN' BILLY, built by Severn Lamb in 1988, heads a train round the lake. 17th May 2015.

ROYAL VICTORIA RAILWAY

Opened in 1996, the 10¼ inch gauge Royal Victoria Railway makes a 1000 yard circuit within the Royal Victoria Country Park at Netley, near Southampton in Hampshire. 6w-6 petrol-mechanical locomotive D1011 WESTERN THUNDERER, built by David Curwen in 1964, heads a train away from the middle station. 3rd May 2009.

RUDYARD LAKE RAILWAY

Opened in 1985, the 10¼ inch gauge Rudyard Lake Steam Railway, near Leek in Staffordshire, runs for 1½ miles from Rudyard Station, on an old standard gauge trackbed, along the side of a lake to Hunthouse Wood. There are intermediate stations at The Dam and Lakeside.

4-4-2 No. 196 WAVERLEY heads away from the passing loop at Lakeside with a train to Hunthouse Wood. This locomotive was built in 1952 by David Curwen, and previously worked at Weymouth, the Great Central Railway at Loughborough, the Dinting Railway Centre, and the Isle of Mull Railway. WAVERLEY arrived at the Rudyard Lake Steam Railway in 2003. 3rd October 2009.

During the 2009 gala weekend, Exmoor Steam Railway 0-4-2T locomotives No. 319 PULBOROUGH of 2004 and No. 334 PEGGY of 2007 approach Rudyard Station with a train from Hunthouse Wood. The locomotives were visiting from the South Downs Light Railway. 3rd October 2009.

DeVere 2-6-2T VICTORIA of 1993 at Rudyard Station. This locomotive previously worked on the Isle of Mull Railway in Scotland. 11th September 2011.

Exmoor Steam Railway 2-4-2T No. 6 EXCALIBUR of 1993 runs off the shed at Rudyard Station during the 2009 gala. Fellow Exmoor Steam Railway 0-6-2T No. 8 KING ARTHUR of 2005 is on the right. 3rd October 2009.

ST ANNE'S MINIATURE RAILWAY

Opened in 1973, the 10¼ inch gauge St. Anne's Miniature Railway, in Lancashire, runs for 700 yards on an oval track at St. Anne's sea front. 4w-4 petrol hydraulic locomotive ST ANNE'S EXPRESS, built by Severn Lamb in 1973, heads a lightly loaded train around the line. 2nd September 2012.

SOUTH DOWNS LIGHT RAILWAY

Opened in 2000, the 10¼ inch gauge South Downs Light Railway runs for 1100 yards within Pulborough Garden Centre in West Sussex. Exmoor Stearn Railway 0-4-2T No. 319 PULBOROUGH of 2004 heads a train past the locomotive depot on 14th June 2015.

A3 4-6-2 No. 4472 FLYING SCOTSMAN stands at Stopham Road station on the South Downs Light Railway. This locomotive was built by J. J. Mahoney in 1935. 9th August 2009.

STAPLEFORD MINIATURE RAILWAY

Built by Lord Gretton and opened in 1958, the 10¼ inch gauge Stapleford Miniature Railway runs for 1¼ miles, with a balloon loop, at Stapleford Park, near Melton Mowbray in Leicestershire. The line is private with occasional open days. Here, 4-4-2 No. 751 JOHN H. GRETTON, previously named JOHN OF GAUNT and built by David Curwen in 1948, stands at the station at the start of the day's services. This locomotive first ran at the Bognor Regis Miniature Railway where it was named CANADIAN CHIEF. It is now fitted with enclosed rotary valve gear. 29th August 2010.

4w-4w petrol-mechanical locomotive No. D100 THE WHITE HERON, built by Curwen and Newbury in 1962, backs on to its train. 29th August 2015.

Based on the East African Railways 2-8-4 Tribal 31 class, No. 3103 UGANDA is seen at work. This locomotive was built by John Wilks in 2008. 30th August 2009.

L.M.S. Jubilee 4-6-0 No. 5565 VICTORIA. This locomotive was built by Richard Coleby and Neil Simkins in 1975. 30th August 2009.

4-6-0 No. 2943 HAMPTON COURT and JOHN H. GRETTON double-head a train away from the station. Based on a G.W.R. Saint, construction of HAMPTON COURT was started by Trevor Guest and was completed by Twining Models in 1939. The locomotive ran at Dudley Zoo until 1944. 30th August 2009.

Nickel Plate Road, New York, Chicago and Saint Louis Railroad 2-8-4 No. 752 at Stapleford. This locomotive was built in 1971 by Richard Coleby and Neil Simkins. 29th August 2010.

Built in 1998 by John Wilks, New York Central 4-8-4 No. 6019 backs out of the station at Stapleford. 30th August 2009.

WATFORD MINIATURE RAILWAY

Opened in 1959, the 10¼ inch gauge Watford Miniature Railway runs for 600 yards in Cassiobury Park, Watford in Hertfordshire. Fenlow 4w-4w diesel-hydraulic locomotive CONWAY CASTLE of 1972 stands on the turntable next to the station. 30th May 2015.

WELLS & WALSINGHAM LIGHT RAILWAY

Opened in 1982, the 10¼ inch gauge Wells and Walsingham Light Railway runs for 4 miles from Wells on Sea station at Wells next-the-Sea, in Norfolk, to Walsingham, with intermediate stations at Warham and Wighton. Built on an old standard gauge trackbed, it is the longest 10¼ inch gauge railway in the world. 0-6-0T No. 1 PILGRIM stands outside its shed at Wells-next-the-Sea. PILGRIM was built in 1981 by David King and hauled the first public trains on the line in 1982. 23rd August 2014.

2-6-0+0-6-2 Garratt locomotive No.3 NORFOLK HERO heads a train to Walsingham, near Wighton, on 23rd August 2014.

10¼ inch gauge 2-6-0+0-6-2 Garratt locomotive No. 6 NORFOLK HEROINE at Wells-next-the-Sea. This locomotive was built by Richard Coleby in 2011. 0-6-0 diesel-hydraulic tram engine No. 2 WEASEL, built by Alan Keef in 1985, is behind. 23rd August 2014.

WELLS HARBOUR RAILWAY

Opened in 1976, the 10¼ inch gauge Wells Harbour Railway at Wells-next-the-Sea, in Norfolk, runs for 1200 yards from Harbour station to Pinewoods. Here, 0-6-0 steam outline diesel-hydraulic locomotive HOWARD, built in 2005 by Alan Keef, heads a train from Pinewoods along Beach Road. 23rd August 2014.

WEYMOUTH MINIATURE RAILWAY

Opened in 1983, the 10¼ inch gauge Weymouth Miniature Railway, also known as the Rio Grande Railway, follows a circular route for 550 yards within Lodmoor Country Park at Weymouth, in Dorset. Here, steam outline 2-6-0 diesel-hydraulic locomotive No.1890, built by Severn Lamb in 1990, is pictured at work. 19th October 2014.

CLEVEDON MINIATURE RAILWAY

Opened in 1952, the 9½ inch gauge Clevedon Miniature Railway makes a 900 yard circuit around Salthouse Fields at Clevedon, in North Somerset. Here, steam outline 2-8-0 petrol-hydraulic locomotive No. 595 CHARLES HENRY, built by Severn Lamb in 1976, heads round the line with a moderately loaded train. The railway has since been converted to 15 inch gauge. 26th August 2012.

BANKSIDE MINIATURE RAILWAY

Opened in 1977, the 8¼ inch gauge Bankside Miniature Railway runs for 300 yards round a balloon loop at Brambridge Park Garden Centre, near Winchester in Hampshire. The track is elevated and the whole train is turned on a 35 foot turntable at the end of each run. There is also a short 7¼ inch gauge ground level track. The only 8¼ inch gauge locomotive at the BMR is 2-6-2T No. 815 CAROLYN, built in in 1924. Here she stands, in the rain, with an empty train at the station. 30th April 2016.

ALL-IN-ONE MINIATURE RAILWAY

Opened in 2000, the 7¼ inch gauge All-in-One Miniature Railway follows a 600 yard circular route around the All-in-One Garden Centre at Allostock, near Knutsford in Cheshire. Here, 4w-4w+4-4 battery-electric locomotive No. 5624/5623, built in 2000 by Express Locomotives, heads a train away from the station. 3rd April 2016.

AVONVALE MES

The Avonvale Model Engineering Society, formed in 2001, operates a 7¼ and 5 inch dual gauge railway at Hillers Farm Shop and Garden Centre, near Alcester in Warwickshire. The railway has a complex layout and is approximately a third of a mile long. 7¼ inch gauge 0-6-0PT No. 2000 LAURA heads a train out of the tunnel. 16th August 2015.

BAGGERIDGE MINIATURE RAILWAY

Operated by the Wolverhampton and District Model Engineering Society and opened in 1997, the 7¼ and 5 inch dual gauge Baggeridge Miniature Railway runs for 300 yards in Baggeridge Country Park, near Dudley in the West Midlands. 7¼ inch gauge 4w-4w petrol-hydraulic locomotive No. 20 BAGGERIDGE RANGER, built in 2005 by the Model Engineering Society, heads a train away from the station. 17th April 2016.

BEER HEIGHTS LIGHT RAILWAY

Opened in 1975, the 7¼ inch gauge Beer Heights Light Railway runs for 1800 yards within Pecorama Pleasure Gardens, near Seaton in Devon. During the 2015 gala weekend, visiting 2-4-2 River Class locomotives No. 2 TARN BECK and No. 1 AFON GLASLYN head a train out of Much Natter station. 26th August 2015.

Semi - resident 0-4-2 FINN MacCOOL, built by TMA Engineering in 1986, heads a train out of the tunnel. 26th August 2015.

Privately owned American outline 2-4-0 ELLA, visiting from Sheffield, with 0-4-2ST No. 4 THOMAS II double-head a train near Deep Water station. 26th August 2015.

BROOKSIDE MINIATURE RAILWAY

Opened in 1990, the 7¼ inch gauge Brookside Miniature Railway is a 950 yard circuit within Brookside Garden Centre, at Poynton in Cheshire. The railway is home to a large collection of standard gauge railwayana. Exmoor Steam Railway 0-4-2T JEAN of 2000 heads a train towards Brookside Central station. JEAN is one of five Exmoor Steam Railway locomotives based on the line. 3rd April 2016.

BROOMY HILL RAILWAY

Operated by the Hereford Society of Model Engineers, the 7¼ inch gauge Broomy Hill Railway runs for approximately 1 kilometre at Broomy Hill, Hereford. There is also an elevated 5 inch and 3½ inch dual gauge railway on the site. 0-4-0ST ELLIE departs from Broomy Hill station, while LILLA waits in the other platform. 27th September 2015.

COALYARD MINIATURE RAILWAY

Opened in 1988, the 7¼ inch gauge Coalyard Miniature Railway runs for 500 yards alongside the Severn Valley Railway, at Kidderminster Town station in Worcestershire. Battery-electric Metropolitan Railway No. 4588 SHERLOCK HOLMES is pictured there. 24th April 2016.

COATE WATER MINIATURE RAILWAY

Opened in 1965 and operated by the North Wiltshire Model Engineering Society, the 7¼ and 5 inch dual gauge Coate Water Miniature Railway runs for 880 yards in Coate Water Country Park, at Swindon in Wiltshire. This fine 7¼ inch gauge model of an ALCo 2-8-2 is pictured approaching the station with empty stock at the start of the day's services. The locomotive is numbered 1942 and carries the name SCREAMING EAGLE. The Eagle above the nameplate is a Harley Davidson motorbike emblem. 8th May 2016.

CONWY VALLEY RAILWAY MUSEUM

Opened in 1979, the 7¼ inch gauge Conwy Valley Railway runs for 950 yards at the Conwy Valley Railway Museum at Betws-y-Coed in North Wales. There is also a 15 inch gauge line worked by a tram. 7¼ inch gauge 0-4-2T DOUGLAS, built in 2004 by P. Frank, heads a train out of the station. The 15 inch gauge line and the mainline station are in the background. 2nd May 2016.

CREWE HERITAGE CENTRE

Opened in 1992, the 7¼ inch gauge Crewe Heritage Centre Miniature Railway is a 600 yard long railway within Crewe Heritage Centre in Cheshire. 4w-4 petrol-hydraulic locomotive Hymek No. D7030 NORCLIFF heads a train into Midge Bridge station. The cab of class 40 diesel-electric 40 088 is in the background. 17th April 2016.

DEVON RAILWAY CENTRE

Opened in 2001, the 7¼ inch gauge Devon Railway Centre Miniature Railway runs for 450 yards round a balloon loop within the Centre, at Bickleigh in Devon. 4w-4 battery-electric locomotive No. D7011, built in 1969 by Cromar White, heads a train out of the wooded section of the line. 21st August 2008.

DIBLEY'S NURSERIES RAILWAY

Opened in 2001, the 7¼ inch gauge Dibley's Nurseries Railway runs for 850 yards in the grounds of Dibley's Garden Centre at Llanelidan, near Ruthin in Denbighshire. The railway is open to the public on occasional running days. Exmoor Steam Railway 0-4-2T CRICOR of 1999 is pictured on 2nd May 2016.

DRAGON MINIATURE RAILWAY

Opened in 1999, the 7¼ inch gauge Dragon Miniature Railway is a 500 yard long, dumb-bell shaped line in the Marple Garden Centre at Marple, Stockport, Greater Manchester. Here, 2-4-2 DANNY, built in 1992 by D. and G. Sims, heads a train away from Otterspool Junction. 3rd May 2016.

There is also a separate short line at the Dragon Miniature Railway, with a tram that children can drive. 4w battery-electric railcar No. 1 TARA THE TRAM, built circa 1990 by R. Kay, waits for her next customer. 3rd May 2016.

ECHILLS WOOD RAILWAY

Opened in 2006, the 7¼ inch gauge Echills Wood Railway makes a 1500 yard circuit, from Harvesters station to Far Leys, within Kingsbury Water Park, at Kingsbury in Warwickshire. There are a number of special events each summer which attract large numbers of visiting locomotives. A fine 7¼ inch gauge model of a Shay geared locomotive is pictured at work during the 2012 narrow gauge weekend. 9th September 2012.

Scenes from the 2015 narrow-gauge weekend. Hunslet 0-4-0ST PENDLE WITCH heads a train of empty slate wagons, complete with a gunpowder wagon, at Far Leys.

Hunslet 0-4-0ST MERLIN runs under the signal gantry at Harvesters with a short train. Both: 19th September 2015.

Scenes from the 2016 standard gauge weekend. A4 4-6-2 No. 4467 WILD SWAN near Harvesters. 16th July 2016.

A fine model of Southern Railway S15 class 4-6-0 No. 837 approaches Harvesters station with a mixed freight. 17th July 2016.

GOLDING SPRING MINIATURE RAILWAY

Operated by the Vale of Aylesbury Model Engineering Society and opened in 1982, the 7¼ and 5 inch dual gauge Golding Spring Miniature Railway runs for 1100 yards within the Buckinghamshire Railway Centre, near Quainton in Buckinghamshire. Before the start of the day's services, an industrial style 0-6-0T heads empty stock away from the carriage shed towards Golding Spring Central station. The elevated track on the left leads to the locomotive preparation area. The locomotive was completed in 2016 and numbers and lettering had not yet been applied. 31st July 2016.

GREAT COCKROW RAILWAY

Opened in 1964, the 7¼ inch gauge Great Cockrow Railway runs for 2000 yards at Chertsey in Surrey. Operated by Ian Allan Miniature Railway Supplies Ltd., trains on this impressive railway start from Hardwick Central and are controlled by three signal boxes. There are two different routes with stations at Everglades Junction, Jungle Halt, Cockcrow Hill and Green Lane. T9 4-4-0 No. 30285 runs round its train at Cockcrow Hill. 2nd August 2015.

Black 5 4-6-0 No. 5241 heads a train under the large signal gantry at Hardwick Central station. 2nd August 2015.

HIGH LEGH RAILWAY

Opened in 2009, the 7¼ inch gauge High Legh Railway is an 850 yard circuit within the grounds of High Legh Garden Centre, at Halliwells Brow in Cheshire. EILEEN heads a train away from the station on the High Legh Railway. 3rd April 2016.

HILCOTE VALLEY RAILWAY

Opened in 1993, the 7¼ inch gauge Hilcote Valley Railway is a 500 yard circuit within Fletcher's Garden Centre at Eccleshall in Staffordshire. The railway was designed and built by Roger Greatrex. 4-4w petrol-hydraulic locomotive Union Pacific No. 6610, built in 2003, also by Roger Greatrex, arrives at the station with a well loaded train. 10th April 2016.

HOLLYBUSH MINIATURE RAILWAY

Opened in 1996, the 7¼ inch gauge Hollybush Miniature Railway is a 950 yard circuit around two lakes at Hollybush Garden Centre, at Shareshill in Staffordshire. Here, 4-4w petrol-hydraulic locomotive No. 645 is seen at work on the railway. This locomotive was built by Roger Greatrex in 1998. 27th March 2016.

The Leicester Society of Model Engineers operates a dual gauge ground level track and an elevated railway at Abbey Park in Leicester. Here, a lightly loaded train approaches the station on the 7¼ inch gauge line. The elevated track is on the right. 14th August 2016.

LITTLE HAY MINIATURE RAILWAY

Opened in 1981 and operated by the Sutton Coldfield Model Engineering Society, the Little Hay Miniature Railway dual gauge ground level railway runs for 2760 feet at Little Hay, near Lichfield in Staffordshire. There is also a 460 foot long elevated railway. Here, 7¼ inch gauge B-B petrol-hydraulic locomotive, Great Northern Railway No. 280A, heads a well loaded train on the ground level track. 29th August 2016.

MILTON KEYNES MES

The Milton Keynes Model Engineering Society operates an oval 7¼ and 5 inch gauge track, 250 yards long, at Caldecotte Lake, Milton Keynes in Buckinghamshire. The society opened the present line in 2010, having moved from another location. There is also an elevated track here. 0-4-2 petrol-hydraulic locomotive HAGRID starts a train away from the station. 6w petrol-hydraulic locomotive No. 8 KATIE, built by M. Hutt in 2008, waits to follow. 7th August 2016.

MIZEN'S RAILWAY

Opened in 2001, the 7¼ inch gauge Mizen's Railway is operated by the Woking Miniature Railway Society. There is over a mile of track and the complex layout sees trains departing from the main station in both directions. G.W.R. 0-6-0PT No. 1504 PADDINGTON, built circa 2011 by S. Conway, stands outside the semi roundhouse at the Mizens Railway. Just inside the shed is 0-6-0T MARQUIS, built by L. Chandler in 1984, next to Roanoke 4w petrol-hydraulic locomotive LEMON of 2004. 8th May 2016.

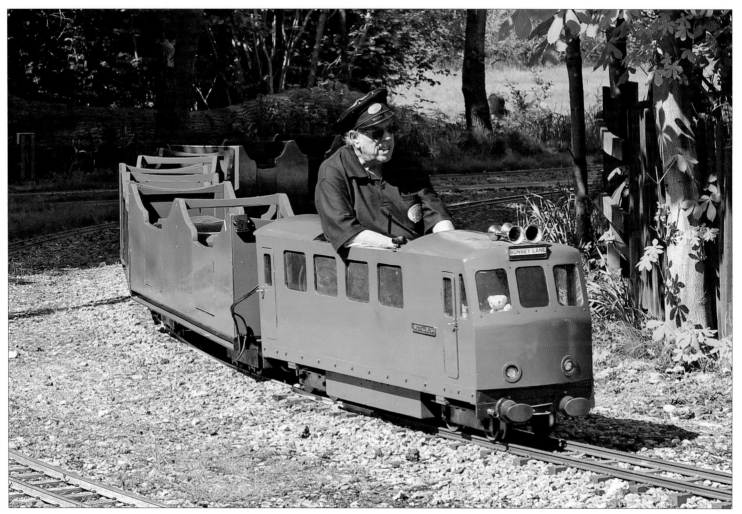

After running round its train on the triangle, 4-4w battery-electric locomotive BROOKLANDS runs back into the main station. BROOKLANDS was built in 1978 by T. Smith. 8th May 2016.

MOORS VALLEY RAILWAY

Opened in 1986, the 7¼ inch gauge Moors Valley Railway runs for 1 mile within the Moors Valley Country Park, near Ringwood in Dorset. Train movements are controlled by two signal boxes and there is a second station at Lakeside. The Moors Valley Railway is currently home to over twenty locomotives. 7¼ inch gauge Tinkerbell type 0-4-2T locomotives No. 3 TALOS and No. 4 TINKERBELL on the turntable during the 2016 Tinkerbell Rally. Both locomotives were built by Roger Marsh, TALOS in 1978 and TINKERBELL in 1968. The Tinkerbell narrow gauge type locomotive was the first 7¼ inch gauge locomotive that the driver could sit in, rather than on. 30th April 2016.

Visiting Tinkerbell 0-4-2T HESTIA at Kingsmere during the Grand Summer Steam Gala. 5th June 2016.

0-4-2T TINKERBELL and 2-4-4T HARTFIELD, built in 1999 by M. Colbourne, double-head a train away from Kingsmere station during the 2016 Tinkerbell Rally. 30th April 2016.

During the Tinkerbell Rally, SARA is prepared for duty at the locomotive depot. HESTIA stands alongside. 30th April 2016.

HARTFIELD waits to back empty stock into Kingsmere station, while CAPTAIN HOOK passes with a demonstration freight train. 0-4-2T CAPTAIN HOOK was visiting the Moors Valley Railway for the Tinkerbell Rally. 30th April 2016.

0-4-2 diesel-hydraulic locomotive No. 2 HORACE shunts a freight train at Kingsmere, before the start of the day's services. HORACE was built at the Moors Valley Railway using a chassis purchased from Roanoke. 30th April 2016.

Visiting locomotive CHRISTINE heads a short train round the long curve on the approach to Kingsmere station. 30th April 2016.

Visiting for the Tinkerbell Rally, 2-4-0T SARA heads a demonstration freight past the carriage sheds at Kingsmere. HORTON is in the background. 30th April 2016.

2-6-2 No. 10 OFFA, built in 1991 by the Moors Valley Railway, heads a train around the long curve on the approach to Kingsmere station. 2nd April 2016.

4-6-0 No. 5 SAPPER passes Kingsmere East Signal Box, as it heads a train away from Kingsmere station. SAPPER was built in 1982 by R. Marsh and J. Haylock. 2nd April 2016.

2-6-2 No. 11 ZEUS heads a train away from Kingsmere station. HORTON stands in the background next to the signal gantry. South African Railways style ZEUS was built in 1991 by A. Culver and the Moors Valley Railway. 29th September 2012.

Based on the class 24 locomotives of the East African Railways, Moors Valley Railway 2-8-0 No.19 ATHELSTAN was built in 2006 by T. Couling. Here, it is pictured at work on the Eastleigh Lakeside Steam Railway during a visit in 2012. 29th September 2012.

4-6-2 No. 12 PIONEER approaches Lakeside station with a train from Kingsmere. PIONEER was built in 1992 by the Moors Valley Railway. 23rd April 2016.

0-4-2T No. 24 PERSEUS approaches Lakeside station with a train from Kingsmere. Enlarged Tinkerbell PERSEUS was built in 2006 by P. Ash and P. Wheeler. 29th September 2012.

2-6-2 ZEUS waits with empty stock as 0-4-2T TINKERBELL and 4-6-0 SAPPER head a train away from Kingsmere station. 5th June 2016.

4-6-2 No.18 THOR shunts empty stock at Kingsmere station. THOR was built in 2006 by Andy Jefford. 2nd April 2016.

RAINSBROOK VALLEY RAILWAY

Opened in 1991 and operated by the Rugby Model Engineering Society, the Rainsbrook Valley Railway is situated in Onley Lane, Rugby, Warwickshire. There is a 1,100 yard 7¼ inch gauge ground level track and a 5 inch and 3½ inch dual gauge elevated track, about 350 yards long. Based on an Orenstein and Koppel narrow gauge locomotive, 7¼ inch gauge THE BARON heads a train into the station. 15th May 2016.

7¼ inch gauge Shay geared locomotive No. 1 IRON MIGHTY rounds the curve next to Onley Lane as it heads a train away from the station. 15th May 2016.

7¼ inch gauge Metropolitan Water Board 0-4-2T HAMPTON heads a train away from the station. 15th May 2016.

SOUTH GARDEN MINIATURE RAILWAY

Opened in 1996, the 7¼ inch gauge South Garden Miniature Railway runs for 150 yards within the National Railway Museum at York. Mardyke 6w-6w diesel-hydraulic Deltic No. 55002 THE KING'S OWN YORKSHIRE LIGHT INFANTRY, built in 2011, is pictured running round its train. 1st October 2013.

Based on the Romulus design, 0-6-0T No. 5 CWECHOLWYN poses for a photograph with a single carriage on the 7¼ inch gauge Steamplates private railway in Worcestershire. 8th August 2015.

SWANLEY NEW BARN RAILWAY

Opened in 1986, the 7¼ inch gauge Swanley New Barn Railway runs for 900 yards from Lakeside station within Swanley Park in Kent. There is also a second station, New Barn Halt, adjacent to the main car park. With the builder in charge, a recently completed class 67 4w-4w diesel hydraulic locomotive heads a train away from Lakeside station. Painted in Royal Train livery, the locomotive is to be named QUEEN'S MESSENGER, No. 67005. 11th September 2016.

6w-6w diesel-hydraulic locomotive HS4000 KESTREL approaches Lakeside station, with a train from New Barn Halt. Based on the 4000hp prototype diesel-electric locomotive built by Brush Traction, this locomotive was built by Mardyke in 1999. 11th September 2016.

WAYSIDE LIGHT RAILWAY

The impressive 7¼ inch gauge private Wayside Light Railway follows a complex route in a mainly wooded area near Maidstone in Kent. It is home to nine locomotives with one diesel. The railway may be visited on occasional open days. 2-4-0 No. 4 WEALDEN LADY heads a train around the curve away from Amsbury Junction. 11th September 2016.

WESTON PARK RAILWAY

Opened in 1980, the 7¼ inch gauge Weston Park Railway follows a dumb-bell shaped route for 1.2 miles from Weston Central station within the Weston Park Estate, near Shifnal in Staffordshire. On a visiting locomotives day, TARN BECK and THE BARON are pictured double-heading a train soon after leaving Weston Central station. 6th May 2012.

WILLEN LAKE MINIATURE RAILWAY

Opened in 1989, the 7¼ inch gauge Willen Lake Miniature Railway runs for 600 yards, round a balloon loop, within Willen Lakeside Park at Milton Keynes in Buckinghamshire. Here, the 4w-4w petrol-hydraulic locomotive, built by F. Kenny in 2001, heads a train into the balloon loop. 7th August 2016.

WOODSEAVES MINIATURE RAILWAY

Opened in 2004, the 7¼ inch gauge Woodseaves Miniature Railway runs for 450 yards within Woodseaves Garden Plants Nursery, near Market Drayton in Shropshire. Here, 0-4-0 petrol-hydraulic locomotive SYDNEY, built in 2003 by Roanoke, poses for a photograph at Woodseaves Junction station. Note the signal gantry with a single arm in the background. 10th April 2016.

KINVER & WEST MIDLANDS SME

The Kinver and West Midlands Society of Model Engineers has operated a miniature railway at Kinver, in Staffordshire, since 1962. The railway today is an elevated 5 inch and 3½ inch dual gauge track, about ½ mile long. There is also a short 7¼ inch gauge ground level track. 0-4-2T No. 3 GIMLI is seen on the 7¼ inch ground level track. 9th August 2015.

5 inch gauge 2-6-0T KWMSME No. 22 heads round the elevated track at Kinver in Staffordshire. A further section of elevated track as well as the 7¼ inch gauge ground level track can be seen in the background. 24th April 2016.

NORTHAMPTON SME

The Northampton Society of Model Engineers operates both raised and ground level tracks at Lower Delapre Park in Northampton. The 5 inch and 3½ inch dual gauge elevated track is 1,740 feet long, while the 7¼ inch gauge ground level track runs for 3,034 feet. Both lines are in a wooded area. The society organises open days once a month during the summer. 5 inch gauge 9F 2-10-0 No. 92220 EVENING STAR heads a train on the elevated track at Lower Delapre Park. 7th August 2016.

TALYLLYN RAILWAY

A short, temporary 5 inch gauge ground level miniature railway, at the Talyllyn Railway's Tywyn Wharf station in Wales, was one of the attractions at the 150th anniversary celebrations of the building of narrow locomotive DOLGOCH. Hunslet 0-4-0ST MAID MARIAN stands on the railway, with Kerr Stuart Wren class 0-4-0ST ROSE OF THE TORRIDGE heading the line up of locomotives alongside. 2nd July 2016.

Worcester and District Model Engineers have operated miniature railways in Worcester since the club was founded in 1946. The society moved to the current site at Diglis in Worcester in 1954, with the present day, 230 yard long, 5 inch and 3½ inch dual gauge elevated track opening in 1999. There is also a 350 yard 7¼ inch gauge ground level track, which was opened in 1968. 5 inch gauge English Electric class 50 No. 50007 SIR EDWARD ELGAR stands in the locomotive preparation area. 16th August 2015.

3½ inch gauge L.N.E.R. V4 2-6-2 No. 3401 BANTAM COCK heads a train round the elevated track. 16th August 2015.

ON DISPLAY

The West Shed at the Midland Railway Butterley, near Ripley in Derbyshire, houses a number of miniature railway locomotives, including Coronation class 4-6-2 No. 6233 DUCHESS OF SUTHERLAND. 17th May 2015.

This fine 5 inch gauge G.W.R. County class 4-6-0 was displayed at the Welland Steam and Country Rally at Welland, near Malvern in Worcestershire. Thirty County class locomotives were built, numbered from 1000 to 1029. This locomotive is numbered 1030 and named COUNTY OF MELIN LLAN, after the home of the builder, Mr. C. H. Burrow. The locomotive was built over a period of thirty years and was completed in 2009. The superbly detailed cab is also pictured. 29th July 2016.

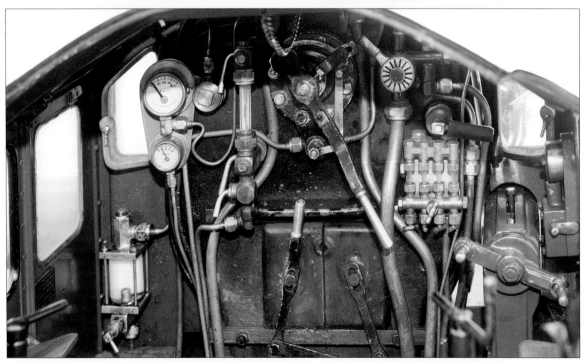

Model engineering allows forgotten locomotives to be brought back to life. This unusual 7¼ inch gauge locomotive was photographed at an open day at Twyford Waterworks, running on temporary track. It is a model of 6-2-0 locomotive LIVERPOOL which was built in 1847 and used on principal express services on the L.N.W.R. 1st June 2014.